Stewards of the Mysteries

CARL E. BRAATEN

Stewards of the Mysteries

Sermons for Festivals & Special Occasions

AUGSBURG Publishing House • Minneapolis

STEWARDS OF THE MYSTERIES

MANUFACTURED IN THE UNITED STATES OF AMERICA

*To my colleagues and students of
The Lutheran School of Theology
Chicago*

Contents

Introduction: On Theology and Preaching

Introduction:
On Theology and Preaching

Theology is the clearing house of sound preaching. Without ongoing critical theological reflection the word from the pulpit is readily ensnared by the latest fads and fashions. Most prevalent today is the psychological captivity of the word of preaching. When psychological jargon gets tedious, the more sophisticated preacher may move on to the latest sociological hypothesis concerning the human predicament. Others, hoping to eschew such conspicuous dependency on the language of psychology and sociology, may rummage around instead in the liturgical esoterica of the past to discover the fine stuff of which sermons should be composed.

We should not underestimate the difficulty of the preacher's task. Anything one must do on a weekly basis cannot be all that simple, if it is meant to arouse the imagination of others. "What language shall I borrow?" I know many preachers experience the misery of a bad conscience. Some of these have had such an abominable experience of theology in seminary, they forget that its chief end is to make preaching possible with a good conscience. Even at best, of course, there are painful tensions between theology and preaching. Theology is a serious business that only a small elite in the church can do very well. Preaching, on the other hand, is bound to be popular; it must somehow reach the masses of people. While we expect preachers to have a solid theological education, they can afford to presuppose nothing of the kind in their audience out there. They have been exposed to the most recent advances in biblical scholarship; most of the laity have not. They have used the critical methods of exegetical scholarship; many lay people don't know they exist. Rather than scandalize the laity with the most shocking results of critical scholarship, the temptation of preachers is to look for easy ways to bridge the gap between theology and preaching. This is why the latest fads and hottest jargon exercise such a seductive appeal.

We have received the message of God's revelation in earthen vessels. The aim of the modern critical historical approach to the Bible is to examine these earthen vessels in every important respect. Most of us, however, are not specialized in biblical scholarship. As pastors we must be jacks of all trades. If we have a field of specialization, it may fall in another area. I happen to have devoted my theological career to dogmatics and systematics. I understand my task as a systematic theologian to be the person at the switchboard who opens the circuits of communication between the exegesis of biblical texts and the meaning of those texts which the church must proclaim to the modern world. The great tradition in the church has always combined the poles of exegesis and proclamation. The dogmatician and the systematician stand between the Bible and preaching. Dogmatics reflect on the church's preaching and aim to regulate it. Preachers are doing dogmatics when they critically ask *what* they are to preach. I would not be a dogmatician at all if I were not concerned about what the church is to preach today, and I would have nothing to preach if I did not think critically about what the church believes. Believing and thinking belong together in both preaching and theologizing. Gerhard Ebeling said it so well: "Theology without preaching is empty and preaching without theology is blind."

Bishops have told me that many of their pastors haven't read a theological book since they left seminary. Evidently theology is seen as an unnecessary detour on the way to the pulpit. Without critical theological reflection what is to prevent preaching from becoming fanatical, unintelligible, irrational and irrelevant? Without taking time for theological reflection, how shall the laity be spared the sermons of overly busy and lazy preachers? How shall they be spared thoughtless speech about God and faith? Critical theology is to serve as the lively conscience of the preacher.

There are different theological theories about what is supposed to be going on in a sermon. I was trained in the classical school of Lutheran homiletics which construes preaching in terms of "law and gospel." I am still committed to this view, only I have transposed it into the scheme of the dialectic between question and answer. Genuine preaching must give an answer—God's answer—to the real questions implied in the human condition. The function of the law is to identify and formulate the real questions, and the function of the gospel is to address them on the basis of the biblical witness. As auxiliaries of the law we preachers are free to use everything in sight—philosophy, novels, magazines, newspapers, personal experiences, etc. Our insights into the gospel come primarily from Scripture, but also from the Christian tradition.

The concept of the law in Lutheran homiletics opens up unlimited access to the widest possible range of human experience in the world in the formulation of the questions, whereas the gospel as answer focuses with the greatest possible fidelity and intensity on God's saving revelation in the person of Jesus the Christ. The priority of the law establishes the point of contact for the gospel. Preaching becomes boring when it fails to deal with real human questions, and it is totally pointless when it provides no answers. That is the essence of the law-gospel distinction, and it conforms very well to the question-answer dialectic in contemporary hermeneutical theory. For all their differences, Bultmann and Tillich were both adherents of this classic pattern in the Lutheran tradition, and I find it still useful in theology and preaching today, even when the old formula of "law and gospel" is not used in so many words.

The style of this book of sermons is to a great extent didactic. This is due in part to the fact that most of these sermons were delivered in the context of congregations which invited a theologian to deliver the sermon on festival days and special occasions. But there is also the fact that in my understanding *kerygma* and *didache* have the identical subject matter. Over the years I have found it quite an easy transition to move from the seminary classroom to the chapel pulpit. There is a real sense in which I must teach doctrine in my preaching, and to preach the gospel in my teaching. For this reason, a friend of mine once remarked, "You couldn't get away with that style of teaching theology in a university setting." Perhaps this is true. I have reason to be grateful that I have been permitted to teach theology in an ecclesial context.

The summer of 1981 in which I assembled and edited this book of sermons marked my twentieth anniversary of teaching systematic theology at the Lutheran School of Theology at Chicago. One previous volume of sermons, *The Whole Counsel of God* (Fortress Press, 1974), emerged out of the same context. I dedicated that book to all the ordained preachers and missionaries descended from the Braaten family in Telemark, Norway. I wish to dedicate this volume to my colleagues and students at LSTC who have heard the greater part of these sermons in the seminary chapel or at Augustana Lutheran Church across the street.

Carl E. Braaten
Chicago, 1981

Part One
FESTIVALS

It's Later Than It's Ever Been!

Besides this you know what hour it is, how it is full time now for you to wake from sleep. For salvation is nearer to us now than when we first believed; the night is far gone, the day is at hand. Let us then cast off the works of darkness and put on the armor of light.
—ROMANS 13:11-12

Advent is here again. We are entering the season of Christmas-card theology. We've all had the experience of trying to pick out the right card for some secular friend, expressing season's greetings—Happy Holiday, Fröhliche Weihnachten, Joyeux Noel, etcetera—without being too explicit about the messianic meaning of the season.

Advent is a season when the church takes four weeks to tell us what time it is—the *kairos* in the world of human events. What time is it? But if you don't know what *time* is, how can you tell what time it is? So this is what Advent is all about: knowing the time, penetrating the black widow's veil which masks the mystery of time. Advent is knowing the time, that now it is high time to wake up. The time of our salvation is near, the night is passing, the day is breaking, so let us walk in the light.

What is time?

There is a mystery about time that even Advent cannot dispel. Christians are as bad off as the philosophers; they don't really know much about the metaphysics of time. With St. Augustine we can perhaps say, "When no one asks me I know. But when I must explain time to someone else, I just do not know." Or, perhaps we know too much about time nowadays. We have clocks and chronometers that measure fractions of seconds with the greatest accuracy. People aren't satisfied to run; they must race the clock. A friend of mine used to run a mile or two every day in the Field House. I asked him if it wasn't boring; "No," he said, "I got a stop-watch for Christmas that helps me keep track of my time."

Our time-consciousness moves from fractions of seconds to the millions and trillions of years we must reckon with, from primeval origins in archeology to the endless vistas of astrophysics. We have become so numb to such inconceivable magnitudes, that if we miscalculate the age of the earth by just a few million years, it doesn't matter, we've come close enough.

I recall a little ditty that puts it quite well:

> There was a young girl named Miss Bright
> Who could travel much faster than light.
> She departed one day,
> In an Einsteinian way,
> And came back on the previous night.

When I was in college, the fashionable thing for the campus intellectuals was to read Aldous Huxley's lusty attack on the tyranny of time in his best-seller, *Time Must Have a Stop*. The basic thought was that we are fools to expect time to deliver up the salvation we need. Doesn't history show that Father Chronos swallows all his children? The poet Baudelaire said it too!

> Time eats up all things alive
> Time blots me out as flakes on freezing waters fall.

Look at all the lively expectations of a Great Advent dashed to pieces against the stone wall of reality. The earliest Christians expected the kingdom. Not even that put an end to time, but gave way to the time of the church and that's not been all that fulfilling even for people who go to church a lot and spend their lives working for the church. Since then history has seen all the noble experiments fail to bring about peace on earth and good will among men. All the efforts to locate the advent of human salvation in time have failed. All the experiments to realize in time a Socratic humanitarianism, a Platonic Republic, an Augustinian City of God, or the Renaissance dream of a New Atlantis or the City of the Sun have failed. All the highest aspirations have remained eternally unfulfilled in time. There's been no great advance in this age in which progress is our most important product. The liberty, equality, and fraternity proclaimed by the French Revolution and taken over by the Founding Fathers into the Constitution of the United States have not come to pass. There has been in fact no irresistible progress from ape to human essence dreamed by evolutionary optimists, no Russian worker's paradise, no land of the free and home of the brave in which the pursuit of happiness is everybody's equal opportunity.

Most people don't expect any great advent of salvation anymore, anywhere, anytime. Lots of people have plunged themselves into pessimism. They are caught in the spider's web of the present and can't get free. With no hope for the future and no power from the past, every moment's got to be charged with the highest voltage. Society holds a whip in one hand and a clock in the other. We have to run faster and faster, making use of every minute, just to keep up with the times, whatever that means.

On the other hand, never before has hard work purchased so much free time, that we moderns have to become ever more inventive in the aimless goal of killing time. This is what Las Vegas is all about.

The Right Time

So what is time, after all is said and done? We don't know, whether the clock time of seconds and minutes, whether the cosmic time of billions of light years, whether utopian time, the future time of our hopes and dreams, frustrated by history and reality, whether the existential time in which every moment is all the time there is, the time to act, the time to choose, the time which can squeeze us to death with an all-oppressive now—in the sense of now or never!

It is into this fallen time in all its dimensions that the eternal God has stepped to bring a new kind of time, the *kairos,* to take time out from his own eternal games to enter the human arena of our lost and failing and broken times. He did it at the right time, the time of the coming of Jesus, born of a woman, born under the conditions of our wretched times. The *kairos* has occurred. Out of the ashes of the old times there arises the phoenix of the new.

What time is it, then, according to the new way of telling time? It is the fullness of time! It is the *kairos!* It is now 1980 *Anno Domini!* That's a little bit of Greek and a little bit of Latin to say that in the coming of Jesus, God has taken time for us. The *kairos* is time seized by the opportunity of God's love. This makes it the fullness of time—pregnant time. If you want to understand time, Tillich once said, don't think first of the time told by the clock.

A newsboy got up early as usual for his paper route, and became perplexed by the striking of the big clock in the living room. His electric clock had read a quarter to six when he got up a few minutes ago. But now the big clock was chiming six, seven, eight, nine, ten, eleven, twelve, thirteen, fourteen, fifteen, sixteen. The boy didn't know that the striking mechanism had gone crazy the night before. So he ran upstairs and awakened everybody in the house as he shouted, "Hurry, get up right away! It's later than it's ever been!"

It's High Time

The New Testament News says that something has happened to human time because of the advent of eternity—God's time. If Advent is the coming of God into human time, if God is taking his time and sharing himself with us, then it is high time for us to do the same, to take time for each other. Advent faith, advent existence, is doing what God has done, taking his own time for others. To take time for another person is to give that person the most precious thing you have. Almost everything else about you is renewable and replaceable. But once time is gone, you can't get it back. There's no reversing the aging process. When time's gone, it's gone forever, and there's only so much of it left for each of us. That's why we want to keep it for ourselves. We don't want to waste any time. That's our strong point. Time is money! Western man has made good use of his time. He's made lots of money. Aggressive, energetic, productive, making full use of the time—these are our strong points. But often it's our strong points that obscure our view of God's coming.

It's high time to take seriously the coming of God in human flesh. "Human beings are the locale of God's coming," says J. B. Metz. He has taken our being and our bodies into his own time. No longer should we live anachronistically as though we did not know the time. Advent means the day is dawning. Put on the armor of light. Walk in the light. "Let your light so shine among men, that they may see your good works and glorify your Father who is in heaven."

It is high time to live as though God's time for us and our time for each other is what human lifetime is all about—namely, that life is a gift with enough time to love. The deepest mystery of time is defined by the outpouring of God's love for us and our spending of life for each other. You tell time not by the clock, though we have to do that too to get on in life. But you really know what time is by what's going on, marked by the crucial events in your life. I asked my son one evening if he knew what time it was. By the tone of voice he knew I meant it was late. "Do you know what time it is?" He replied with a question, "No, what time is it?" I said, "It's ten o'clock, time for the news." And budding theologian that he is, he knew that for him that meant past his bedtime.

"For everything there is a season, and a time for every matter under heaven" (Eccles. 3:1). The same preacher who said that long ago said, "Ah, but all is vanity." Listen to the pairs of contrasts:

> a time to be born, and a time to die,
> a time to weep, and a time to laugh,
> a time to mourn, and a time to dance,
> a time to embrace, and a time to refrain
>   from embracing,
> a time to keep silence, and a time to
>   speak,
> a time for war, and a time for peace.

There's a time for all things under heaven. But it can all be in vain. "Vanity of vanity, all is vanity," saith the preacher. True, perhaps, except for Advent, except for letting God's time enter our circles of vanity, letting all our moments of time, letting all our toiling and planning, letting all our comings and goings, point to the right time, the fullness of time, the Advent of God's eternal time breaking into our human timing of things.

There's a time for everything. But it's a question of timing, of getting your timing right, of getting in step with the Advent of God's timing for all things under heaven.

If you're tuning up a car, it's a question of timing. If you're hitting the ball, you want your timing to be perfect. If you're meeting a train, your timing had better be in line with the schedule. There's also a *kairos* in your life.

I've often had the urge to go into one of these houses on Stony Island, or 95th Street, where there's a sign that says, "Reader and Advisor." These people are experts on the right time. They can read your chart or your palm or maybe tea leaves, for all I know. They know there's a right time, the appointed hour.

For creatures of Advent there's no need to consult such oracles. There is the one great *kairos*. And because of that, every time becomes the right time for God's time! Every moment can be your *kairos*, to take time for others. Like a stick put into the water, it curves away from the perpendicular line. So it is with the *kairos* of God's coming in Christ. It comes down and is bent in the direction of others, making every time a chance to bring more light and love into our human world. That's the good news of Advent and our hope for Christmas!

Nazareth Was a Hick Town

In those days a decree went out from Caesar Augustus
that all the world should be enrolled. This was the first
enrollment, when Quirinius was governor of Syria. And
all went to be enrolled, each to his own city. And
Joseph also went up from Galilee, from the city of
Nazareth, to Judea, to the city of David, which is called
Bethlehem, because he was of the house and lineage of
David, to be enrolled with Mary, his betrothed, who
was with child. And while they were there, the time
came for her to be delivered. And she gave birth to her
first-born son and wrapped him in swaddling cloths,
and laid him in a manger, because there was no place for
them in the inn.

—LUKE 2:1-7

Familiarity blinds us to the meaning of words and symbols that
reach us from the past. Oftentimes our religious traditions and
ritual repetitions cover up statements of revolutionary meaning.
The whole story of Christianity in history began with Jesus of
Nazareth. *Jesus of Nazareth*—the name of a person and his

22

hometown. But there's more to it than such matter-of-fact infor-
mation you expect to find in a book of history—names and places
and dates and all that stuff. To be sure, we have to get our
history straight, also with respect to our Christian faith. That's
because, as theologians never tire of saying, Christianity is a historical religion. It's bound up with real facts of history. But
there's more than meets the historian's eye. These facts are
loaded with meanings.

Just take the name "Jesus." Some parents look in a book of
names, and choose a couple that sound just right. Joseph was
visited by the angel Gabriel who said, "You shall call his name
Jesus, for he will save his people from their sins." That's a great
name. It means "savior." But a lot of Jewish boys at that time
were named Jesus. It was a common Jewish name. So it is necessary to be still more specific and identify *which* Jesus we mean.
We mean Jesus from Nazareth. And what's so important about
Nazareth? Nothing! Nothing at all! And that's just the point
of the message of Christmas. The entire gospel of God is packed
into that seemingly simple straightforward historical identifica
tion of a man and his hometown: *Jesus of Nazareth.* Here is
where history and faith meet. Here is where the gospel of the
humility of God became wrapped in the swaddling clothes of
historical facts. Consider the irony of the Christmas story: the
heavenly Son of God hails from a dirty little village somewhere
in the Mid-East.

Nazareth hasn't changed much in the last two thousand years.
We've been to Nazareth and looked around and have to say:
Nazareth was a one-horse town if ever I've seen one. But that
was Jesus' hometown. It's almost unbelievable that something of
such world-historical meaning as the gospel of our salvation
should have been conceived in this little jerkwater town, first
in the womb of Mary, and then in the heart of Jesus. The whole
gospel of the New Testament hinges on this incidental fact of
history.

Nobody important ever gets born in Nazareth. Very often we let the gospel take its shape solely around the climactic events of Jesus' death and resurrection. We call that the gospel of the "double ending" of Jesus' life: his cross and his resurrection. But there is also gospel at the very beginning, at the point of his origins. The end without the beginning would not be the whole story; the beginning without the end would be pointless. All the beautiful talk about Christmas, the incarnation in the royal city of Bethlehem, all the heart-warming stories about the wisemen, the shepherds and the angels, would be nothing but fairy-tales without the crisis and catastrophe of the cross. In a certain sense the end is like the beginning. The *humility* of God stands at the beginning of the story, and his *humiliation* at the end. All the joy of Christmas and Easter should not be allowed to cancel the good news of God's humility coming down to earth in that insignificant little city where Jesus grew up as a boy.

Nazareth was hardly a little speck on the map and had nothing in it to make a person naturally proud of calling Nazareth his hometown. So Jesus left Nazareth, after spending his youth there and his early manhood as a carpenter. He became an itinerant preacher. One day he came back to Nazareth and went to church. He had meanwhile acquired some fame as a preacher and as a healer. He was beginning to get a following. You would think that the people in Nazareth would be happy to see him come home again. But the homecoming was disappointing. He offended the village leaders and the church people, because as he read from the Bible, he finished with the comment: "Today you have seen Scripture being fulfilled before your eyes." I'm the one whom the Scriptures are pointing to. And the people got mad. Jesus—just the kid next door—everybody knows who you are! What kind of a messianic pretender do you think you are? You're the carpenter, Mary's son and the brother of James and Joseph and Judas and Simon, and we know your sisters too.

That's when Jesus said, "A prophet is without honor in his own town and among his own people."

There was common tradition which held that when the Messiah comes, nobody will know where he comes from. He'll just appear, like a man from outer space. So people debated whether Jesus could possibly be the Christ, because he's just the ordinary blue collar worker whom everybody remembers growing up in Nazareth. But when the Christ appears, they said, no one will know where he comes from. If Jesus is the Messiah of God, then he cannot be Mary's son and Simon's brother—speaking the local dialect shared by us all. People expected the Messiah to come zooming down from heaven, speaking more the language of an angel from heaven than one of the Nazareans of despised Galilee.

What is the point of insisting on Jesus' humble and lowly origin—his coming from a town that's hardly a speck on the map? It had always been that way with Jesus. He was born in a stable and cradled in a manger. That's like being born in a little straw hut in the squalor of a slum, because there was no room in the better hotel on main street. Jesus was not able to gain any credentials, either from his birth or his bringing up. His parents were not important people. They had no economic affluence, no political clout, and no social status to speak of. The neighbors, you can be sure, kept whispering about the fact that Jesus—after all—was an illegitimate child. Of course, the stigma of his birth was later covered up by the liturgical confession that Jesus was born of the Virgin Mary—who appears almost like a goddess from heaven. That sounds sweet compared to what the boys called Jesus on the playground. Which is to say that Jesus had a tough bringing up, starting from nowhere.

Isn't that very much like the stories of other religious heroes—who are born of peasant stock and rise to fame as religious geniuses? Don't we thrill to hear about Jesus as a kind of religious success story? Jesus—of humble birth—born in a stable but in the end exalted, even sitting gloriously at the right hand of the Father? But the story of Jesus is so different. This is not the usual scenario of the success story—from rags to riches, from a slum shack to a rich man's palace. The difference is that when Jesus leaves his home town, he is *forever* the Man of Nazareth. He does not change his name or cover up his identity, and get himself a nice place to live in the better part of town. He continues to identify himself with the poor. Not like the new rich who, when they get theirs, forget their origins in poverty, and turn their backs on their own kind of people. Our ordinary human way is to celebrate the self-made man who begins from scratch and claws his way to the top, earning the luxury—the privilege—to forget all the little people at the bottom. But Jesus is so different. He leaves his home town of Nazareth, and forever bears the marks of his humble origins. He is never too good for the kind of forgotten and insignificant people he grew up with. To keep his identity as the Man of Nazareth meant to let the love of God shine on the human face of poverty, and to share his identity with all the nameless nobodies who come and go on the stage of history.

Jesus did not go around apologizing for being the Man from Nazareth. He never bragged about it, but he didn't let it bind his freedom. It became the launching pad for his ministry of sharing the blessings of the kingdom with a strange crowd of poor and sick people, lepers and tax collectors, Samaritans and sinners, women and children, all the kinds of people who were usually bypassed by the political establishment and the religious professionals . . . such important people who thought they were just an inch away from the kingdom of God.

But Jesus brings about a new definition of the kingdom of God, by tying its coming to himself as the man from dinky Nazareth and bringing its power and glory to the side of the very marginal people in society. Poor, weak, and bent over, wretched people of the earth—what can we do about them? They are all known by this Man from Nazareth and they are to be remembered and given top priority by this man's mission. Insignificant nobodies, the nameless and faceless individuals who are just numbers in a teeming mass of humanity, they are all infinitely valuable as they are touched and named one by one and as they enter a new family of persons, in which God is Father, and Jesus is their everlasting friend and brother.

God himself has tied his own eternal reputation to the Nazarene origin of Jesus. In the Nicene Creed, we confess that Jesus is God of God, Light of Light, Very God of Very God, but these beautiful words were not laid on him in his lifetime. He was the humble man from Nazareth, no halo to mark him off from the ordinary village people. He did not come as a God, as the celebrated founder of a nice new religion. In Chicago we have a new religion, this one, believe it or not, imported from India. It was introduced just a few years ago by a roly-poly teen-age boy. They call him a god—Maharj-ji. The media, newspapers and magazines, always looking for a new sensation, have given this god an illustrious welcome. It's the kind of success story that fits into the American dream. A teenage hero, marrying an American beauty, owning a couple of Cadillacs, amassing a few million dollars, and gaining thousands of followers and devotees. It is called The Divine Light Mission. Jesus enters the stage of human history in a totally different way.

Jesus gave us a new and paradoxical definition of God, a definition of the humility of God. Many people were offended. They wanted a God of glory, not entering the world at the bottom, not from a despised place like Nazareth in Galilee, but he must come in from the top. He must be properly introduced, by the right people, and with the appropriate protocol. But, instead the people got the Man from Nazareth, and he was only prepared to give them a message of the humility of God, of the identification of God with people and things that don't count for very much in this world. He carried this message to the extreme, driving the humility of God all the way to the cross. It was a scandal, to have the Messiah come from Nazareth; it was even a worse scandal that he would get nailed to a cross, and die like just another convicted felon along the road outside the gate.

The Christian faith has been erected on the scandalous origin and destiny of Jesus of Nazareth, in our history, in our world. It just can't be that the Messiah should come from Nazareth, that such a prophet could rise up from Galilee; it just can't be that the meaning of God would be incarnationally bound to the pattern of this life and its movement from poor little Nazareth in Galilee to the humiliating cross in Jerusalem. The story of the incarnation, from beginning to end, spells out in the life of Jesus, God's own will and willingness to be involved in the common lot of human experience, even sharing his life with the wretched of the earth. This is the story of one man starting at the bottom, and getting to the top, to be sure, but it was the top of a hill where he dragged the rugged cross on which they hanged him. He didn't die with a sword in his hand, using the instruments of violence to advance his cause. But he died an ignominious and unheralded death, one of the three criminals on that spot. If we want to look for the meaning of God, then and there, as well as here and now, we have somehow to look for the clues in the story of the Man from Nazareth, who was destined to live out the poverty of his origin in solidarity with the wretched of the earth, all the way to the bloody cross, in order to show forth the humility of God, his down-to-earth love, and his total commitment to the calling of God's kingdom, to bring salvation to the sinful and liberation to those in bondage.

Of course, now Nazareth is on the map. Lots of tourists flock to see it. But it's still a little village. It still bespeaks eloquently the humility of God who came to a little hole of a place on earth, not to a royal palace, so no matter who you are or where you come from, he has reached all the way down. The humility of

God has made contact with the humiliations of humanity, in the person of Jesus. And we can enter into that experience, in the liberating event by which God's incarnation in Jesus shows itself in Jesus' solidarity with the unwanted, the untouchables, the abused and the rejected people of his time. That's what Jesus of Nazareth is all about. That's the meaning of "Nazareth" in world history.

If, as the followers of Jesus, we become Nazarenes, it means we take up the cross. We share the message of the humility of God and bring the leverage of his incarnate love to the help of the humiliated people of our time, in whatever way we find an opening to do so.

True and False Praying

"Beware of practicing your piety before men in order to be seen by them; for then you will have no reward from your Father who is in heaven. Thus, when you give alms, sound no trumpet before you, as the hypocrites do in the synagogues and in the streets, that they may be praised by men. Truly, I say to you, they have their reward. But when you give alms, do not let your left hand know what your right hand is doing, so that your alms may be in secret; and your Father who sees in secret will reward you. And when you pray, you must not be like the hypocrites; for they love to stand and pray in the synagogues and at the street corners, that they may be seen by men. Truly, I say to you, they have their reward. But when you pray, go into your room and shut the door and pray to your father who is in secret; and your Father who sees in secret will reward you."

—MATTHEW 6:1-6

One of the signs of stress in our day is that busy people are turning to meditation to calm their nerves and recollect who they are. People are not flocking to the temples to pray, but they are searching out masters in the art of meditation, gurus who can teach them yoga techniques and the secrets of Zen.

I met a friend the other day who dropped out of the seminary a few years ago. He told me that now he was into TM, and that it had made him feel like a new man inside. Rarely have I heard a Christian speak of the meaning of prayer in such glowing terms.

Penitence and Prayer

As we enter the season of Lent our thoughts turn to penitence and prayer. Thus it is a dangerous time of the year for Christians. Jesus taught his disciples to pray, but he saved his most scathing condemnations for people who made praying into a profession, whether in the streets or the synagogues, whether in the pious platitudes of the Pharisees or the empty phrases of the Gentiles. Lent is a dangerous season for Christians, especially for priests and pastors and seminarians too, because they are tempted to make it one of their professional competences, one of the items on a list to be checked off.

What can we do? We pray under the law, but reaching out for the kingdom of God. So it was in Jesus' time, and so also in ours. We pray—perhaps I speak for myself—sometimes out of a sense of duty. It comes hard. We'd rather do almost anything else in the world. But then sometimes we pray out of desire, a longing for the kingdom of God, the soft breathing of the Spirit within, a time of closeness to God, confidence and clear vision.

Who is it that stands in the place of the hypocrite today? Is it the person who prays out of a sense of duty? I think not. Jesus is not placing a high premium on praying just when and as we feel like it. He is no romantic. He is not getting on the Pharisees because they are struggling to fulfill the law, or because they are working hard in prayer to bring in the kingdom of God.

Phony prayers

Yet, nothing irritated Jesus so much as phony praying. One way of praying—ancient and modern—is that of self-indulgence, praying to make oneself feel good, to get an emotional high. When you get carried away and are gushing emotions all over the place, go lock yourself up in a closet and tell it to your Father.

Another way of phony praying, as we know from experience, is self-serving, trying to make a deal with God. Here it's not so much feeling good, but getting something for nothing, or at least cut-rate for being such a good Christian. So Jesus said, if you do something good to get a reward, some people might be impressed by that, but your Father sees into your foolish heart.

A third phony kind of praying is self-righteous, making a great show of eloquence. Here it's not so much feeling good or getting something cheap, but making pretty phrases to reflect one's advanced state of sanctification.

Of such phony praying, Jesus said, "You hypocrites! You are like white-washed tombs that look handsome on the outside, but inside are full of dead men's bones and every kind of corruption. In the same way you appear to people from the outside like good honest men, but inside you are full of hypocrisy" (Matt. 23: 27-28).

So, if Lent is a time for us to turn on the praying, like a spigot of running water, we are entering a very dangerous zone. We are playing with a poison, potentially harmful to the human soul, otherwise Jesus would not have made it the most earnest subject of his warnings and teachings.

Authentic praying

So how shall we pray? Jesus never said, since praying is so dangerous, try the more harmless techniques of transcendental meditation. We are given some clues, both from the teaching of Jesus and the tradition of the church. The church has said, "pray in the name of the Father, the Son and the Holy Spirit." The Christian prayer is trinitarian, marked by three meaningful words: Abba—Amen—Alleluia. Jesus himself used these words, full of meaning and power. "And Jesus said, 'Abba, Father, all things are possible to thee.'" (Mark 14:36a) And Paul said, "And because you are sons, God has sent the Spirit of his Son into our hearts, crying, 'Abba! Father!'" We have some inkling of the meaning of "Abba." It's the Hebrew diminutive meaning "daddy." If you have a son or a daughter you know "daddy" is the most intimate word of affection you can hear. By this word we look away from ourselves, and we look for the face of our Father, or at least a strong hand to hold us!

Jesus also used the word "Amen." Heinrich Schlier, a Roman Catholic New Testament scholar, says that Jesus' use of "Amen" contained the whole of Christology in a nutshell. And here, too, Joachim Jeremias says we see packed into this single word the consciousness of Jesus' own authority. So when we pray in the name of Jesus, we say "Amen; so let it be!" Let it be according to his will, and not according to my self-indulging prayer, my self-serving and self-righteous phony ways of praying. So the book of Revelation calls Jesus "the Amen" (Rev. 3:14). Jesus is the faithful and true witness, the beginning and the goal of God's creation. So we don't pray poking around into our soggy subjectivity, looking there for a solid ground of confidence, but our trust and hope lie in the power of the great name, the "Amen" of the heavenly Father, the One who lets the God of the universe and the God of his people become our God.

And in addition, we would not have truly caught the spirit of prayer in the New Testament without the note of joy and praise, the "Alleluia" of the great liturgies of the church that mean, "praise Yahweh." As we begin Lent we are straining forward to hear the mighty "Hallelujah Chorus."

It is only through the Spirit that we can sing praise unto God, and say "Jesus is Lord." "Alleluia" (1 Cor. 12:3). It is only by the Spirit that we can be released from our own phony praying, that we can be delivered from rummaging around in ourselves for life and salvation, and turn away from ourselves, crying out "Abba, Father!" "Amen. Come Lord Jesus!" "Alleluia!" Salvation and glory and power belong to our God, for his judgments are true and just. . . . Alleluia! For the Lord our God the Almighty reigns. Let us rejoice and exult and give him the glory (Rev. 19:1b and 6b).

Born in an Upper Room

Then came the day of Unleavened Bread, on which the passover lamb had to be sacrificed. So Jesus sent Peter and John, saying, "Go and prepare the passover for us, that we may eat it." They said to him, "Where will you have us prepare it?" He said to them, "Behold, when you have entered the city, a man carrying a jar of water will meet you; follow him into the house he enters, and tell the householder, 'The Teacher says to you, Where is the guest room, where I am to eat the passover with my disciples?' And he will show you a large upper room furnished; there make ready." And they went, and found it as he had told them; and they prepared the passover. And when the hour came, he sat at table, and the apostles with him. And he said to them, "I have earnestly desired to eat this passover with you before I suffer; for I tell you I shall not eat it until it is fulfilled in the kingdom of God." And he took a cup, and when he had given thanks he said, "Take this, and divide it among yourselves; for I tell you from now on I shall not drink of the fruit of the vine until the kingdom of God comes." And he took bread, and when he had

35

given thanks he broke it and gave it to them, saying,
"This is my body. But behold the hand of him who be-
trays me is with me on the table. For the Son of man
goes as it has been determined; but woe to that man by
whom he is betrayed!" And they began to question one
another, which of them it was that would do this.
— LUKE 22:7-23

Communism was born in a London library, as Karl Marx de-
veloped a theory of revolution for the liberation of the proletarian
masses of industrial Europe. Christianity was born in an upper
room, where Jesus met with his disciples to eat the passover, to
prepare for his suffering, to share the cup and break the bread
which was to become the feast of thanksgiving—the eucharist—
in which Christians in whole continents and entire centuries re-
mote from that Last Supper would continue to meet Christ.

It happened in an upper room . . . away from the public. Christianity was born in secret. It began with Jesus, and with a hand-
picked team of very close friends. It began away from the crowd,
off the streets, without publicity and newspaper reporters to
broadcast the secret meeting the next day. It was like the birth
of Jesus in that respect—a humble beginning, born in a barn, no
room in the Holiday Inn. This founding event of Christianity
took place in an upper room, not in a science laboratory; within
a closed circle of intimate friends, not in the academy of learned
men, on the occasion of eating and drinking, not in meeting to
make big plans for the future and political schemes. This meeting in the upper room with Jesus is a necessary reminder to us
that Christian faith contains something hidden, secret, arcane; it
contains mystery, miracle and ecstasy which only faith can
understand. Christian faith is not a public philosophy of religion
and morality which any two-bit rationalist can boil down to a
system of clear and distinct ideas.

One would think that a dinner party with one's closest friends would be the definition of joy and happiness. Not so with Jesus. His heart was heavy with sorrow and suffering. Why? There was not a lot of joking and laughing and story-telling at that supper. This was the last supper. This was a foretaste of the suffering to come on the cross. In just a few hours now Jesus was to become the political football of the Jews and the Romans. Too hot to handle for the Jews, he was kicked over to the Romans; too hot for Pontius Pilate, he was handed over to Herod. But that's not what was bothering Jesus. He could handle the Romans. He had a deeper problem, and that was God, his Father, the one whose kingdom he had lived to inaugurate.

Jesus was looking for the coming of God's kingdom. He had preached the kingdom; he believed he had the powers of the kingdom. He believed he had the Spirit, to heal, to forgive, to make the kingdom come near to sinners, to poor people, and to the minority groups of that time. But now the crunch. Now the moment of truth. Would God really bring in his kingdom? Or would Jesus be frustrated in his life's calling? Would Jesus be disappointed? Would Jesus who worked for God be forsaken by him when it counts? It's enough to make us mad. . . . God luring Jesus into the work of the kingdom, and then leaving him in the lurch. So would Jesus have to suffer for nothing? Would he have to suffer all alone? Is there anybody in the world who could understand the dilemma of Jesus? Parents, brothers, sisters, friends, students, anybody? Or would Jesus head into this trial all alone, bearing the sins of the world, carrying the cross of the kingdom on his back, sweating drops of blood on his bewildered brow? Would all this suffering for the kingdom be in vain? Would his ministry for righteousness, truth and love be a miscarriage of zeal? What if the kingdom didn't come? Would Jesus have lived his life in vain? This was suffering of the soul; the thorns and the nails were soon to come. This was a suffering between Jesus and God, between the Son and his Father, and nothing the Jews and the Romans could do would go so deep.

Add insult to injury. Jesus was bent low by the thought that soon he would be betrayed. Not even his own team would stand up for his kingdom rights. First Judas, then Peter, and at last all the rest were about to betray him and the cause for which he struggled. And what was that cause? It was the righteousness of God's kingdom, that it might come to sinners, to make them clean. It was the riches of the kingdom, that it might come to poor people, to fill them with good things. It was the freedom of the kingdom, that it might come to people in bondage. It was the light of the kingdom, that it might come to blind people. It was the health of the kingdom, that it might come to lame, sick, and crippled people. That was the cause; it was a good cause. And now both God and his friends were about to abandon and betray him, not to mention the priests and the politicians, the fickle crowd and the murderous mob. Jesus felt himself to be all alone.

Had we been there, would we have stuck up for Jesus? Would we have taken his side? We are always taking sides. Is it the side of the strong against the weak? Is it the side of the righteous people against the sinners? Naturally, we like to think we take the side of the underdog against the bully.

It happens often that when I watch an athletic contest, I'll immediately start pulling for the underdog. But then I'm a mere spectator. It doesn't cost me anything. But in taking Jesus' side, it will cost you your life. If you do not deny yourself, you cannot be the disciple of Jesus. There's a bit of Judas and Peter in everyone of us. Woe to the person by whom Jesus is betrayed. For then we have dropped the cause for which he struggled; then we have left Jesus alone, to his own grief and sorrow and suffering.

This meal is a test of discipleship. Jesus gives himself to us, his body and his blood, and we are asked whether we shall share his cup of suffering and the blows to his body for the sake of the cause to which he surrendered his life in absolute devotion and obedience. This was a meal in which Jesus was struggling for the meaning of his career. Had he missed his calling? It's rather late to discover in your early thirties, that you're in the wrong profession, that you've wasted your life.

The next day the news would be flashed across the networks of that time. Jesus has been condemned by the Jews as a blasphemer of God, and by the Romans as a rebel. People will say that he got his just dessert, or that he was a victim of his own zeal—like Che Guevara, the Castro revolutionary gunned down in Bolivia. Either he got what he deserved, or he let his idealism get the best of him.

But the trial of Jesus was only externally a trial before the Jews and the Romans. On the inside it was a trial of his soul before God. Jesus was on his way to the cross. He was pausing for this last meal. He was a tortured soul. Socrates died a calm and cheerful death. He gave a marvelous farewell address. He felt like a free man. He had a cock sacrificed to Asclepius, which was only done when a person became free, or recovered from an illness. The death of Socrates was an escape to freedom.

But Jesus was struggling in these last hours. He was a man of grief, of sorrow and suffering. He had fought for a cause, but he was not sure now that God would honor it by bringing in the kingdom.

This way to the cross was not like the death of a martyr. The martyrs died knowing they were right. They believed that if they died, their cause would triumph in the end. But not so with Jesus. If he should die, that would end the cause for which he lived. Then everything has been in vain, down the drain, all for nothing. And wickedness and sin and poverty and oppression will continue in the world as before. And nothing will have been changed for the better, if he should die and the kingdom not come.

But Jesus was on his way to the cross, not like a Socrates and not like a martyr, and not to die a cheerful and honorable death, but an ugly, unhappy, despicable and disappointing death. Let's not beautify this suffering, this betrayal, this way to the cross. This was no banquet, no feast, no rollicking good time with a bunch of friends. The soul of Jesus, we are told, was greatly distressed and troubled, sorrowful even unto death. Soon there would be loud cries and tears. Soon he would cry out, "My God, my God, why hast thou forsaken me?"

Let's remember Jesus. Let's leave it at that for now. Let's remember the man of sorrows stopping for a meal on the way to the cross, suffering the bitterness of a soul being forsaken by God, left to suffer and die for sins he did not commit, left to struggle for the kingdom without the power of God to vindicate him, left to die on the cross all alone.

Who Put the Roses on the Cross?

For the word of the cross is folly to those who are perishing, but to us who are being saved it is the power of God.

—1 CORINTHIANS 1:18

Then Jesus was led up by the Spirit into the wilderness to be tempted by the devil. And he fasted forty days and forty nights, and afterward he was hungry. And the tempter came and said to him, "If you are the Son of God, command these stones to become loaves of bread." But he answered, "It is written, 'Man shall not live by bread alone, but by every word that proceeds from the mouth of God.'" Then the devil took him to the holy city, and set him on the pinnacle of the temple, and said to him "If you are the Son of God, throw yourself down; for it is written, 'He will give his angels charge of you,' and 'On their hands they will bear you up, lest you strike your foot against a stone.'" Jesus said to him, "Again it is written, 'You shall not tempt the Lord your God.'" Again, the devil took him to a very high mountain, and showed him all the kingdoms of the

41

*world and the glory of them; and he said to him, "All
these I will give you, if you will fall down and worship me." Then Jesus said to him, "Begone, Satan! for
it is written, 'You shall worship the Lord your God and
him only shall you serve.' " Then the devil left him,
and behold, angels came and ministered to him.*

—MATTHEW 4:1-11

The Sign of the Cross

From the very beginning the cross has been the chief symbol
of the Christian faith. If you were an archeologist digging up
some ancient ruins and you came upon the symbol of the cross,
you could conclude that Christians had left their mark. If you're
driving along and see a distant building displaying a cross, you
know it's a Christian church. If you are in a strange land and
come upon a group of worshipers speaking a foreign language,
and you see the priest dismiss the assembly with the sign of the
cross, you know immediately they are Christians. When I was
in Jerusalem during Holy Week I saw Christians following in
the footsteps of Jesus doing the stations of the cross.

The apostle Paul said, "The word of the cross is the power
of God unto salvation."

Two thousand years ago a cross was raised against an Eastern
sky, and from a distance you would have been able to see a tiny
insignificant speck of a human figure pinned to that cross. Con-
sidering the tremendous achievements of Greek philosophy and
Roman law, nobody would expect much of world-historical
meaning to be happening on that day just outside the gate of
Jerusalem. Not too many days after that seemingly unimportant
event, a handful of men and women began to announce the
cross as the axis of world history, and the person on that cross
as the hope of the future, more important than Greek philosophy,
or Roman law, or Jewish prophecy, or Hellenistic mysteries.

Paul was a man who knew about all these things, and yet he

preached the word of the cross. But it wasn't easy. The intellectual elite of that time were in search of the good, the true, and the beautiful, the highest possible goals of human aspiration. Paul felt there is something silly, downright foolish, about preaching the cross as the hope of all humanity. There is something scandalous and shameful in talking about the cross. There is something ugly, unaesthetic, unrespectable and shabby about the word of the cross. It wasn't easy to preach the word of the cross as the power of God unto salvation. It was felt to be in bad taste.

The Rosy Cross

As time went on Christians began to feel that the rough wood of the cross could be beautified and made smooth and serve as an emblem of the triumphal destiny of the church among the rulers of world history. If Christianity was to become the victorious religion of the empire, either we get rid of the cross or we cover it up with jewels and roses. Well, we can't get rid of the cross. That's here to stay.

When Victor Hugo, the great French author, died, the French decided to secularize the Pantheon, to tear down the great gilt cross that loomed like the Eiffel tower into the Parisian sky. A Christian orator stepped forth to protest this action, but he did not carry the sympathies of his audience. Indignantly he cried, "You think you can take away the cross from the Pantheon." They screamed, "We have taken it away. We've torn it down." And he shouted, "You'll never take away the cross from the Pantheon." They shouted, "It is taken away, and down with the church." When the shouting stopped, he quietly said, "You cannot take away the cross from the Pantheon, for the Pantheon is built in the form of a cross, and when you have taken away the cross, there will be no Pantheon anymore."

We cannot take the cross out of Christianity, because then it won't be Christianity anymore. But we can do something else. We can turn the cross into something nice. We can put flowers and jewels on the cross. We can make a valuable cross of silver and gold and wear it as an ornament.

The German poet, Goethe, wrote a little poem in *Die Geheimnisse,*

> There the cross stands, thickly wreathed in roses.
> Who put the roses on the cross?
> The wreath grows bigger, so that on every side
> The harsh cross is surrounded by gentleness.

So who put the roses on the cross? We all do. Our tradition has done it. Theologians do it, when they try to explain the cross in a way that completely fits into our systems of religious doctrine. Priests do it, when they integrate the cross into a triumphal procession of glamorized religious ceremonies. Pious lay people do it, when they superstitiously use the cross as a thing of magic.

Who put the roses on the cross? We all do it. It's the biggest cover up in world history.

The Crux of Religion

We preach the word of the cross as the power of God unto salvation, the cross of the man who was crucified not symbolically between two nice candles on an altar, but concretely between two thieves in the place of the skull outside the gates of the city. That cross of Jesus was the crucifixion of his own temptations to turn his status as Son of God in history into a lofty position of power and privilege.

If you are the Son of God, you don't have to go the way that leads to the cross. You can use your identity to turn these stones into loaves of bread. If you're so great, you may have acquired such a bag of skills and tricks, that you can do almost anything on your own power and authority.

If you are the Son of God, you can plunge into some foolish experience, and you can trust that in the crunch God will bail you out. Because you are a religious person you can be foolhardy, indolent and unprepared and pass it off as faith and trust in the loving care of your heavenly Father.

If you are the Son of God, you can expect to be great and gain some glory from your religious position. As a person with some impressive religious credentials, you can expect to be treated with deference and dignity, and placed on the roster of those who rule and make very important decisions about other people's lives.

Now the point of the cross in Christianity is this: it is the crucifixion of the worldly way of being religious. It is the crucifixion of the spiritual lust for power, privilege, and glory. It was the temptation of Jesus. It is our temptation today. It was Jesus' acceptance of the way to the cross that put an end to his temptation. It is the cross that spells liberation from the lusts of religion, from the temptation to turn our office of ministry into a stepping stone of progress. It is the cross that frees us from rummaging around for recipes of success. It is the cross that gives us the courage to face the truth, that reveals the blasphemy of playing games with our calling. It is the cross that makes us eternally suspicious of the idols and taboos and fetishes that hide within our religious practices.

I would like to close with some words that I have often quoted from Dietrich Bonhoeffer: "God lets himself be pushed out of the world on to the cross. He is weak and powerless in the world, and that is precisely the way, the only way, in which he is with us and helps us. Christ helps us, not by virtue of his omnipotence, but by virtue of his weakness and suffering . . . Only the suffering God can help. . . ."

The Easter Game

•

And when the sabbath was past, Mary Magdalene, and Mary the mother of James, and Salome, bought spices, so that they might go and anoint him. And very early on the first day of the week they went to the tomb when the sun had risen. And they were saying to one another, "Who will roll away the stone for us from the door of the tomb?" And looking up, they saw that the stone was rolled back; for it was very large. And entering the tomb, they saw a young man sitting on the right side, dressed in a white robe; and they were amazed. And he said to them, "Do not be amazed; you seek Jesus of Nazareth, who was crucified. He has risen, he is not here; see the place where they laid him. But go, tell his disciples and Peter that he is going before you to Galilee; there you will see him, as he told you." And they went out and fled from the tomb; for trembling and astonishment had come upon them; and they said nothing to any one, for they were afraid.

—MARK 16:1-8

At a rally sponsored by the Communist Party in modern Rus-
sia, the speaker was eloquently pronouncing the death of God
and debunking the myths on which the Christian faith is based.
After his presentation the crowd was silent. Then the voice of
an elderly man shouted, "Christ is risen!" One by one the crowd
joined in the exuberant Easter response of the Russian Orthodox
Church, "He is risen indeed."

I am not sure it's good for the soul, but this year I re-read the
classic proofs that the resurrection of Jesus Christ is a fraud.
Some of them are serious; some are downright funny. Not to
torture our souls, but to test our faith—our faith—it is good to
remember that a lot of bright and beautiful people don't look at
life in the light of the Son—S-O-N—who rose on Easter morning. There are variants of the joke about the cardinal calling the
Pope in panic, and asking, "What'll we do for Easter? they've
found the body!" Even in the somber days of Lutheran Orthodoxy, which is well known for its lack of humor, we are told,
Easter sermons used to begin with a joke. I guess it's true, if you
can't joke about something deadly serious, there's not much
freedom and joy in it; you're still sitting in the tomb of gloom
and guilt.

It would be fun to share our favorite jokes about Easter.
There's a clue in Matthew that even in the earliest days, stories
were circulating that the disciples came by night and stole the
body away. That's the theft theory. Then there's the theory of
mistaken identity. As the women were jabbering, they got confused, came to the wrong tomb and found it empty. When the
gardener said, "He is not here; Come, see the place where they
laid him," the women became frightened and ran away. Then
there's the swoon theory. Even some well-meaning rationalists
like Renan have said that Jesus fainted on the cross, but later
revived in the cool cave, and quietly disappeared. And perhaps
most popular of all is the theory, that out of those wrenching
emotional trials of passion week, the closest friends of Jesus

hallucinated and believed they could still feel Jesus alive. They pulled a rabbit of faith out of a hat of fear.

The Easter story is still a challenge to critics and skeptics, historians and believers. They are puzzled by a mass of contradictions on everything, including people, time, place, manner, viewpoint, language and sequence. Even expert news reporters would have their hands full trying to put together the events of those final days.

And now for the message from our sponsor: the New Testament is the New Testament and not the Old, because Jesus was raised from the dead. An astounding miracle, unlike any other miracle that could ever occur, except one. And that's the creation of the world out of nothing. If reporters had been there when the world began with their cameras and note pads, God only knows what a jumble of contradictions might have resulted. Well, the resurrection is the first event of the new world on the other side of death. And for that we have no analogy. We have only the story and the experience of faith and the history of Easter celebrations and the witness of martyrs. And there just isn't going to be another way to find out; there won't be, there cannot be a reopening of the investigation that could lead to a cock-sure certainty and put an end to the need for struggle and faith. So this is the message from our sponsor—the story of faith and the history of Eucharist.

Jesus Christ emerged from the tomb and goes before us to make all things new. He emerged from the tomb to break open the vicious cycle of endless and monotonous repetition. The greatest rival to Easter is the myth of eternal return. It's to be found in most world religions. Life goes in a circle, where every end brings you back to the beginning again. You find it so eloquently stated in Ecclesiastes: "There's nothing new under the sun." Every creature is pinned to the wheel of reality that goes round and round. We've all had perhaps the eerie feeling of déjà vue; we've been here before. Well, Easter tells us it's not so.

Chrysippus, a Greek philosopher said, "Socrates and Plato will exist again. Everyone will suffer the same and do the same thing again. Every city, every village, and every field will grow again, and this will happen not once, but in an endless repetition." The early Christians broke away from this eternally rolling wheel of existence, because they believed Jesus emerged from the tomb of the dead, never to return again. He goes before us to make all things new, never to grow old again. So neither are we xerox copies of anything that ever existed before.

It's anything but an Easter view of life when James Joyce in *Finnegan's Wake* constructs the whole novel as an accumulation of repetitions. The book never really ends; for the last sentence flows right back into the first sentence of the book, which begins not at the beginning but in the middle of things.

It's true that in America we make buying new things our national sport. The government gives us tax rebates hoping we'll go out and buy new things to keep the wheels of the economy rolling. All our pay checks rest absolutely on this compulsion to get something new. I'd be a liar if I told you that I'd rather drive an old jalopy than a new car. But we're all tired of buying new things that don't work like new, but fall apart in a day or two. Our mad pursuit of novelty in a throw-away society isn't deeply satisfying. Having a lot of new things doesn't make us feel really new. We don't become new. The New Testament says, because of Easter we will become new and all things will become new: a new covenant, new tongues, a new commandment, a new name, new wine, a new creation, a new heaven, a new earth. For Jesus emerged from the tomb in which the old gets buried, and he goes before us to make all things new.

Easter newness liberates us from the fetishism of novelty—though as American Christians we don't act very liberated. We also make a fetish of fashion and the latest things; the new look, the new model, the new trend, the new morality, the new theology, to tickle our fancy for novelty. But all that new stuff leaves everything radically the same. It all gets old and puts us under the deadening weight of all the new junk. No one but the Old Adam in us gets much of a thrill out of it. Haven't you had the feeling, when you've gone out to buy something new, that it's really not the new thing you need, but to see things with new eyes? Haven't you had the experience when traveling to get away, to see new places, that everything would be so much better if only you could bring new eyes or a new outlook. If only the gleam of Easter could be in your eye!

Einstein said, "We all hear the same things. Only our ears are shaped differently." We all live in the same world. We can either let the Easter light of the new world shine into the darkness of the present time, or we can crawl back into the tomb, wrap ourselves and sit there corpse-like, in grave clothes, all bogged down in yesterday's problems.

Jesus emerged from the tomb, and he goes before us to make us free. He leads the procession of humanity to freedom. Easter spells fredom. It is God's revolution against the powers and principalities that enthrall us. Death is swallowed up in victory. O, death where is thy sting?

But Easter freedom does not let us escape from the world. Just as Easter newness reaches us in the midst of a world cluttered with old and decadent things, so also Easter freedom still involves suffering and struggle, still a sharing in the cross of Jesus. For the powers that crucified Jesus still hold sway in our lives. The happy freedom of Easter is tempered by the pain of Christ in a world so full of suffering.

The secret of Easter joy is that when freedom cannot be realized, it can still be celebrated. And that is what the joy of the Easter Eucharist is all about.

In a moving report from a South American jail, we are told about the tens of thousands of political prisoners. Here some

Christians found themselves on Easter Sunday. What does the resurrection of Jesus Christ say when you have lost your liberty, and life itself becomes precarious and uncertain? In this report, a priest tells how a score of Christian prisoners experienced the freedom of Easter in a celebration of communion—without bread or wine. The non-Christians gathered around them, making a curtain to block the view of the guards. Any meeting, except for informal conversation, was severely punished. "We have no bread, and not even any water to use in place of wine, but we will act as though we had," said the priest. "Like when we were kids," said a boy of 19 who had joined a team of militants, and now was condemned for thirty years. "You know that Christ told us to act with the simplicity of children. So he will accept our celebration." The lack of bread which they experienced became a sign that the risen Christ is present also among those others outside who lack bread and who are thirsty. They experienced this celebration as a hope, even as a move toward the liberty they were being denied, as one more step in the long march to justice.

This is what it means: the freedom of Easter can be celebrated, in the midst of captivity and the struggle for liberty. The tomb of Christ burst open from the impact of new life it could not contain, giving us a sign and a promise that even prison walls will crumble at the force of faith and the communion of freedom no one can snatch from those who celebrate the presence of the risen Christ in the world.

When we were kids, we played church too. Someone would be the preacher, someone the sexton to ring the church bell, another to take up the offering, and a couple others to sit in the pews looking miserably pious. I'm sure my dad, who was a preacher, must have thought we were taking a mocking attitude to what he deemed most serious.

But that is something like we are doing in the celebration of newness and freedom at Easter. We are only playing a kind of game, as though we were already in the kingdom of God, on the other side of this world of bondage and death. We are celebrating freedom and newness, as conditions of the future kingdom, while we still live under the rule of the powers that put Jesus to death. We are playing the Easter game, and it has nothing to do with bunnies and eggs. At Easter we pick up the refrains of the choirs of heaven, and join in singing a free song of praise. We join in the laughing of the redeemed and the dancing of the liberated, even though we will live under the same old and deadly conditions of last Friday, conditions under which even God is suffering great pain for a broken and bleeding humanity.

The game of Easter calls us to play the role of conquerors, while we are still being conquered; to play the role of victors, while we are still the victims; to play the role of those who have entered the heaven of liberty, while still in bondage, to make a mockery of the powers that rule this body of death, to thumb our nose at the evils that run riot in the land, to take a mocking attitude toward sin, and death, and hell and wrath and all the demons of damnation that make our souls and bodies sick, that still subject our world to suffering.

The Easter game is therefore tense with contradiction. So full of joy, so full of pain; so close to heaven, so close to hell; the empty tomb is not far from the cross; the garden not far from the hill; only three days and a ten minute walk. "When freedom draws near the chains begin to hurt." Those who leap for the joy of Easter also bend low at the pain of this world and the suffering of people. But it is this tiny glimpse of the future that Easter brings, a foretaste of joy and victory, and an eternal celebration of redeemed life, that gives unconquerable hope in the midst of the dark ages—that gives hope that God can take what is weak, and broken and good for nothing, that God can take the crucified, the outcast and the damned, and make us all free and new. For Easter happened in a graveyard. That's

the precedent on which we bank our hopes. Resurrection takes
place in the midst of the dead. There's the promise by which
we live. The Lord of life has emerged from the tomb, and he
goes before us. Christ is risen! He is risen indeed! Amen.

This Side of Easter

Therefore the Lord God sent him forth from the garden of Eden, to till the ground from which he was taken. He drove out the man; and at the east of the garden of Eden he placed the cherubim, and a flaming sword which turned every way, to guard the way to the tree of life.

—GENESIS 3:23-24

If for this life only we have hoped in Christ, we are of all men most to be pitied.

—1 CORINTHIANS 15:19

Martin Heidegger, the German philosopher, characterizes the human situation in terms of "being thrown into the world." Thrown into the world, literally headfirst, we eventually crawl to our feet, and begin to ask, "Where in the world are we? What time is it?" We spend the rest of our lives trying to find out. Here at the seminary we study theology, we learn the practice of ministry, because we believe we have some answers to those questions, "Where in the world are we? What time is it?" Our answers come from the Scriptures.

We are just outside of Eden, but on this side of Easter. Everything else in the Bible is just filling in the details. But you wouldn't know it if someone hadn't told you. You are just outside of Eden. You've been driven out. You're not sitting in paradise. Outside of Eden everyone is confused; people are struggling just to survive, just hanging on. But Eden has left its mark on your memory. We live and work somewhere in a field of thorns and thistles, somewhere between paradise lost and paradise restored. That's why we're not satisfied where we are. Our hearts are restless. There's no place between Acapulco and Hyde Park that will ever be fully satisfying. That's why we hunger not only for bread, but for absolute meaning. That's why we long not only for a few slices of life, but for the whole loaf of its fulfilling meaning. That's why we look beyond our immediate environment and call out to the mystery we cannot see; and call it "God."

We cannot go back to Eden. The gate is guarded by a flaming sword. We cannot go back; we must go forward. We cannot hope to regain a paradise for ourselves anywhere just outside of Eden. We can move around in the ghettos and out to the suburbs of Eden; we can drive ourselves nuts grubbing for the good life. We can and we should join Mayor Jane Byrne's campaign to clean up this filthy city. We can and we should join the struggles of the liberation movements, to create the widest range of freedom and justice possible for all people.

But look, we don't live anymore only outside of Eden. We live on this side of Easter! And that puts a different light on things. If our hope in Christ is good for this life only, and no more, then we deserve more pity than anyone else in the world. Because of Easter the hope we have in Christ cannot be fulfilled by cleaning up the environment around Eden.

My wife has a nice suburban lady working in her store who says she has never been to Chicago. She is satisfied in the suburbs. There are people, aggressive with hope, who act valiantly to change the social system, to overthrow political tyranny, who protest forms of injustice in South Africa or South Chicago. Christians among them. But if we think we can produce the new reality, the new world, for whose coming Christ died and was raised again, we Christians are the most pitiful people in the world.

It was outside the gate of Eden that the hope of humanity was put to death, nailed to a cross, then placed in a grave. It was amidst the dead and discarded heap of humanity that a new and true and finally fulfilling hope for the world was born from the grave.

Christianity was born from that resurrection, born to become its own kind of liberation movement in the world. There's no other liberation movement like it. All the others are committed to a better life for a certain constituency in this or that corner of the human community surrounding Eden. That's important. But we should not go at it as though we live on the wrong side of Easter, as if that's all the hope we have in this life. Christianity becomes pitiful, we become pitiful Christians, the moment we live outside of Eden as though Easter never happened. If we live outside of Eden, but on the wrong side of Easter, it's easy to sink into despair when the movements on which we banked our hopes are smashed. Our dreams turned into the ashes of disillusionment, our hopes to despair; our winning streak comes to an end, and we don't know how to live as good losers; because winning at the expense of others is the name of the game in all the neighborhoods around Eden. When things get really tough, we look for a scapegoat, somebody or something on which to blame all our troubles. It's capitalism, or it's communism, or creeping socialism; it's blacks or it's whites; it's the first world or the second world; it's the Arabs or a Jewish conspiracy; it's a problem of class, or race, or sexism. A spokesman for a middle-eastern despot was asked why so many people were being tried and shot without due process of law, without the right of appeal.

He answered, "The revolution is still in progress and it must run its course." From the deposed leader's tyranny to the people's revolution—that's par for politics in the jungles of life outside of Eden. The counsel of Caiaphas can still be heard: "It is expedient that somebody should die for the people."

St. Augustine said, "Our whole faith is founded on the resurrection of Christ. Greeks and Jews and others know about the death of Christ. But Christians alone believe in his resurrection."

But how pitiful, if believing in the Lord's resurrection, we hope only for this life, hope only to change a few things in the ghettos and outlying suburbs around Eden, but then like everyone else we live on the wrong side of Easter. The challenge to Christianity, to the church, its mission in the world and the everyday life of Christians, is how to bring the hope of Easter into the context of life outside of Eden, how to mingle our absolute hope in Christ with our modest hopes for change and the betterment of human life here and now. For this is also most certainly true: "If our hope in Christ is good for the next life only, and no more, then we deserve to be pitied." But in fact, ours is a total hope, an all-inclusive hope—a hope for this world and also for the mystery of life beyond.

Who's in Charge Here?

In the first book, O Theophilus, I have dealt with all that Jesus began to do and teach, until the day when he was taken up, after he had given commandment through the Holy Spirit to the apostles whom he had chosen. To them he presented himself alive after his passion by many proofs, appearing to them during forty days, and speaking of the kingdom of God. And while staying with them he charged them not to depart from Jerusalem, but to wait for the promise of the Father, which, he said, "you heard from me, for John baptized with water, but before many days you shall be baptized with the Holy Spirit." So when they had come together, they asked him, "Lord, will you at this time restore the kingdom to Israel?" He said to them, "It is not for you to know times or seasons which the Father has fixed by his own authority. But you shall receive power when the Holy Spirit has come upon you; and you shall be my witnesses in Jerusalem and in all Judea and Samaria and to the end of the earth." And when he had said this, as they were looking on, he was lifted up, and a cloud took him out of their sight. And while they were gazing

into heaven as he went, behold, two men stood by them
in white robes, and said, "Men of Galilee, why do you
stand looking into heaven? This Jesus, who was taken
up from you into heaven, will come in the same way as
you saw him go into heaven."

—ACTS 1:1-11

There was an altar painting in one of the churches I recall on
the mission field. The Malagasy artist no doubt copied his pictures from one the missionaries had given him. It shows some
clouds, and beneath the clouds a couple of feet dangling still
visible, and the disciples standing around peering up and looking
gaga. The story of the ascension was built into the whole narra-
tion of the Son of God coming down from heaven, being born
of a virgin, living a human life, then crucifixion and resurrection,
and after forty days, appearing now and then to his friends, he
ascended to heaven and still sits at the right hand of the Father.

In the heyday of Bultmannian demythologizing, I was in
Heidelberg, Germany, and I recall the headline of a church newspaper editorial: "Himmelfahrt, ohne Himmel?" The point was,
if we demythologize heaven, then where did Jesus go on Ascension Day?

When I was a seminary student, there was a campus debate
on the proposition, "There's no place like hell." The fundamen-
talist side was arguing, heaven and hell must be particular places.
The Bible says so. The other side was arguing, No, these are
spatial pictures to depict existential states of being. The debate
came to an end when we all graduated.

To tell the truth, these two elements in the creed, "He ascended into heaven and sits at the right hand of the Father," have
been much neglected in the church, and not only in the church
but in theology. We have so much trouble catching the existential thread of relevance in these pictures of Jesus going up
through a cloud and sitting now at the right hand of the Father.

What is the existential question? What does it all mean for us today? Think of it this way. The ascension is like the punctuation mark in a story. It is a transition. It marks the end of one chapter, and the beginning of a new one. It is the end of the time in which Jesus would be revealing himself on earth, according to the flesh, and the beginning of the time when he would convey himself through the Spirit.

If we ask, "Where did Jesus go?" We can only answer, "He went to the Father." He returned home. He had come into a far country. Karl Barth said, "The ascension means coming home, homecoming for the Son."

Didn't that leave the disciples in the lurch? But Jesus said, "It's to your advantage that I go away." That's like saying, you're better off without me, from now on.

So it seems the disciples are left to run around Jerusalem, Judea, Samaria, and to the far corners of the earth, while Jesus is sitting around in heaven, at the right hand of the Father. Even Luther said it's a silly picture, if you take it literally like Zwingli did. Jesus sitting up there in heaven, while we are racing around down here on earth.

But Luther said, the right hand is a symbol of power, exercised in the name of the highest ruler. If Jesus is at the right hand of God almighty, he is in charge. Zwingli argued that since Jesus is in heaven, he cannot be really and wholly present here in our midst today. Luther said, he sits at the right hand of the Father. It means the exact opposite of what it seems to say to our literal-istic rationalistic minds.

When Jesus went away, the community of believers he left behind said, "He's still in charge." He sits at the right hand of the Father. That means in spite of what seems to be the case, he's really in charge. He has moved to the position of dominion and glory and honor and power over all things in heaven and on earth. It's a grand statement of faith contrary to all appearances, against the way things seem to the naked eye.

The early believers had the same question we still ask. Who's running things anyway? Who's in charge of life and history and the trends of the times? Who's in charge of Washington these days? Who's in charge of our foreign policy? Harry Truman used to say, "The buck stops here." That's what it means to confess that Jesus sits at the right hand of the Father. He's in charge, even now.

Returning by plane from Geneva a few years ago, I found myself sitting next to an Iranian architect, now living in exile in Italy. We spoke openly and freely about the situation in Iran, the government, the Shah, the Ayatollah, the hostages. And he said, the trouble is that no one is really in charge. It's a mess. It's chaos. There's no clear authorized center of power. But there are lots of usurpers and pretenders.

That's what the early Christians said too. Jesus has been exalted to the position of power. He rules by divine right. But there are still many usurpers. We won't bow to them. Jesus is Lord, and he's the only Lord—and to all the rest we'll give only what's due.

During Hitler's time, the Confessing Church led by Karl Barth wrote the Barmen Declaration, which confessed the One Lordship of Jesus Christ, and there can be no other *Führer* in an ultimate sense. So Barth and Bonhoeffer and Tillich and Niemöller and Piper and many others opposed Hitler, because Jesus is Lord, the one and only Lord. All others are usurpers, if they demand our complete allegiance and obedience and claim to be in charge of our lives and souls.

Jesus sits at the right hand of God. He's got the whole world in his hands. First, he's got the right and the power to rule in the church. This is the rule of Christ according to his grace and gospel through Word and Sacraments in the church and for the church. There can be no other ultimate ruler in the church and over the church, no absolute lord or bishop or pope or book or dogma or constitution. There is one Lord Jesus Christ who rules the church, and he has not abdicated the throne to anyone else.

Anyone who says otherwise is a usurper and a false prophet—the Anti-Christ in the church.

Second, Jesus sits at the right hand of the Father, and that means he's active also outside the church! His lordship is not restricted to the church. The old saying that he has no hands but ours, no feet but ours, no voice but ours, is simply not true! Beyond his spiritual rule in the hearts of believers, beyond his rule in the church through Word and Sacraments, his claim to lordship reaches the outer circumference of creation, touching everything that lives and moves in nature and history. All powers are subject to the lordship of Jesus Christ. After all, it's a grand homecoming, this ascension to the right hand of God. For all things were created through Christ; the Father was not alone. All things were created for Christ and find their meaning and goal in him.

You can just imagine the early Christians, martyred in the colosseum and crouching in the catacombs, asking, "Who's in charge?" And then confessing, in spite of everything, Jesus Christ is Lord. He is at the right hand, above all powers, principalities, angels, thrones, dominions, authorities, eons. All the pretentious rulers of history and humanity—they are far beneath the throne to which Jesus has been raised to the position of glory and power and dominion. All the super-powers directing nations, all the world-rulers in charge of empires, political, economic, social, national, and international, all of these puffed up hierarchies are no match for the lordship of Christ, who sits at the right hand of the Father.

But, of course, let's be honest, it doesn't look that way. The lordship of Christ is hidden, even from the eyes of faith. It's not apparent! You can't read about it in the news. It's contrary to the facts. Instead of lordship, there is still suffering and humiliation and crime. Each week the police blotter reports the crimes even in our own neighborhood, the burglaries, holdups, purse snatchings, rapes, and murders. Multiply that by millions of times and you see a world writhing in the grip of evil powers, while it seems the Lord is on a holiday, sitting around in heaven looking the other way.

No wonder the saints have cried out, "How long, O Lord!" How long will it be before you take charge and show the world the substance of your claim to Lordship, so that it's not just the empty rhetoric of pious people? How long, how long before you return in your glory, and put all the enemies in the world at your feet? How long before all of us who are kept hostage by sin and death and the powers of evil, become delivered, become free at last?

He ascended into heaven and sits on the right hand of the Father. But that's not all. He will come again with glory to judge both the living and the dead. At last his kingdom shall have no end. For he shall reign for ever and ever. That's the way it is, according to the Christian faith.

Divine-Human Solidarity

And when he [Jesus] had said this, as they were look-
ing on, he was lifted up, and a cloud took him out of
their sight. And while they were gazing into heaven
as he went, behold, two men stood by them in white
robes, and said, "Men of Galilee, why do you stand
looking into heaven? This Jesus, who was taken up
from you into heaven, will come in the same way as you
saw him go into heaven."

—ACTS 1:9-11

The Ascension of Jesus Christ is one of those events that took place on a weekday and therefore usually gets ignored in churches where the liturgical life is only a leap from Sunday to Sunday. In addition to this quirk of the calendar, there are other reasons why the ascension has never really become top priority in Christian worship and doctrine. The first is that Luke is the only one to tell the story of the ascension. We don't find it in Paul or John or Matthew or Mark or anywhere else in Scripture.

The second reason is that at first sight the ascension doesn't seem to fit the faith. For the story says that Jesus went away and left his disciples behind. But he also said—in the very last verse of Matthew—"I am with you always until the end of the world." Zwingli, Luther's great opponent, loved this ascension story, because in depicting Jesus as physically taken up into heaven, it proves that he is not really here on earth anymore. Whereas Luther was teaching the real presence of Christ sacramentally in the bread and wine, Zwingli was teaching the real absence of the body and blood of Christ, according to the picture of a physical ascension.

A third and a more modern reason that people don't want to bother with the ascension is that it is bound up with a childish picture of the universe. People of those days, even their wisemen and scientists, pictured the world like pre-schoolers of today. For them heaven is the upper story of the universe, and the ascension is literally a flight into space. It was not uncommon for a great person, especially if he claimed to be a son of God, to be snatched from the earth by a whirlwind. Especially philosophers and emperors, like Romulus, would be taken up in a cloud and swept into heaven by a whirlwind. Such an idea of going up into heaven like Dorothy in the *Wizard of Oz* doesn't fit our modern picture of the world in which there is no above and no below.

There were two men in white robes that day, and they said to the disciples, "Men of Galilee, why do you stand looking up into heaven?" In the seventeenth century, these two men in the white robes were the theological inquisitors of Pope Paul V. They used this verse to refute the disciples of Galileo who were teaching the new heresy, the Copernican view of the universe. "Men of Galileo," they punned, "why stand ye gazing up into heaven?" Here the Bible, the Word of God, offers proof positive that heaven is a space above us and despite that modern heretic, Copernicus, ours is a triple decker universe.

If we carry on along this track we will find no gospel in the story of the ascension. We will miss the point that Luke is trying to convey, a message that has to do with faith and salvation.

The first point in this story of salvation is that the ascension is the exaltation of the Son of man. But before the exaltation there was the humiliation of the Son of God. "Who, though he was in the form of God, did not count equality with God a thing to be grasped, but emptied himself, taking the form of a servant, being born in the likeness of men" (Phil. 2:6-7). This is the incarnational curve, the Son of God becoming a human being, so that as God in the flesh he can exalt the human nature of humanity. In this we have the gospel of human dignity. The humiliation of God has brought dignity and glory and honor to our human being. This is the unshakeable basis for saying, as Jesse Jackson teaches his people to say, "I am somebody." I may have a good job, lots of money, and a big name, but if I don't have an inner sense of dignity and if I lose sight of the majesty of being human, then I am of all people most wretched. Let us remember the exaltation of the Son of man, who clothed himself in our human nature, to make it his own temple forever as he goes to the right hand of the Father.

Secondly, the man who is being exalted is the One who has just been through hell. In taking upon himself our human nature, he discovered the tragic sense of life, the meaning of being lonely, forgotten and even Godforsaken. He became obedient unto death, even death on a cross. Then, our creed says, "he descended into hell," there to suffer the pain of our human separation from God at its uttermost extremity.

The One who is being exalted in the ascension went through hell on earth those last miserable days of his life. He was accused of blaspheming the holy name of God with whom he knew himself to be in perfect harmony. He was rejected by the professional interpreters of the law of God, then crucified by the Romans, and died completely abandoned by his God and Father.

The One who suffered the hell of separation from God did not travel that route for himself alone, but he made the cry of every person in the world his very own. He took upon himself the wretchedness of every person who is going through hell today, the hell of suffering, violence, rape, torture, hunger, disease and mental breakdown. The One who is being raised on high is the One who was bent down low in death, even the despicable death on the cross.

Thirdly, as Jesus goes to the Father he did not leave the disciples like orphans in the world but he called them to be his witnesses. "But you shall receive power when the Holy Spirit has come upon you; and you shall be my witnesses in Jerusalem and in all Judea and Samaria and to the end of the earth" (Acts 1:8). The ascension is the end of the forty days when Jesus appeared to his friends as the risen Christ. In just a few more days we have Pentecost, the day this tiny little Palestinian sect became a world missionary movement, so that Christianity today is the only truly global faith. From the ascension to the final advent of Jesus Christ is the time for mission. If we orient our life and thought between those two points, we always know what time it is. We never know when the end is coming, but we know that it is now high time for the members of the body of Christ to follow their Head. As he said, "Go, make disciples, baptize and teach."

The ascension means, then, that Jesus goes to the Father to share his dominion over the whole creation, to lead the procession of the world home to its everlasting future and fulfillment. But as he goes he sends. He sends his Spirit to fire up the church at Pentecost. And as the Spirit comes we are sent, so we go and tell what we know of God's coming in the flesh, the humiliation of the Son of God and the exaltation of the essence of being human.

When our systems of society put a cheap price tag on human life, when people are caught in the vicious circles of decadence and death, when the more defenseless—the unborn babies, the unwanted children, the forgotten old people, and the wrong kinds of refugees—have too few to speak up for their humanity, then there is One who represents them before the Father. There is One who lifts them up and exalts them to the highest heavens. For the ascension is not the story of how Jesus left us behind at the hands of our enemies. It is the message of the solidarity of God with humanity in Jesus who took upon himself our nature and promised to share his destiny with the humanity of every person.

Where and When the Spirit Blows

*When the day of Pentecost had come, they were all to-
gether in one place. And suddenly a sound came from
heaven like the rush of a mighty wind, and it filled
all the house where they were sitting. And there appeared to them tongues as of fire, distributed and resting
on each one of them. And they were all filled with the
Holy Spirit and began to speak in other tongues, as the
Spirit gave them utterance. Now there were dwelling in
Jerusalem Jews, devout men from every nation under
heaven. And at this sound the multitude came together,
and they were bewildered, because each one heard them
speaking in his own language. And they were amazed
and wondered, saying, "Are not all these who are speaking Galileans? And how is it that we hear, each of us in
his own native language? Parthians and Medes and
Elamites and residents of Mesopotamia, Judea and Cap-
padocia, Pontus and Asia, Phrygia and Pamphylia,
Egypt and the parts of Libya belonging to Cyrene, and
visitors from Rome, both Jews and proselytes, Cretans
and Arabians, we hear them telling in our own tongues
the mighty works of God." And all were amazed and*

perplexed, saying to one another, "What does this mean?" But others mocking said, "They are filled with new wine." But Peter, standing with the eleven, lifted up his voice and addressed them. "Men of Judea and all who dwell in Jerusalem, let this be known to you and give ear to my words. For these men are not drunk, as you suppose, since it is only the third hour of the day; but this is what was spoken by the prophet Joel: 'And in the last days it shall be, God declares, that I will pour out my Spirit upon all flesh, and your sons and your daughters shall prophesy, and your young men shall see visions, and your old men shall dream dreams; yea, and on my menservants and my maidservants in those days I will pour out my Spirit; and they shall prophesy. And I will show wonders in heaven above and signs on the earth beneath, blood, and fire, and vapor of smoke; the sun shall be turned into darkness and the moon into blood, before the day of the Lord comes, the great and manifest day. And it shall be that whoever calls on the name of the Lord shall be saved.' "

—ACTS 2:1-21

Something happened on the Day of Pentecost, and we cannot be sure what it is. We are told what it was like. It was like being engulfed by a gale of wind and a rain of fire. It was like being blasted by the breath of God, blown by the winds of excitement beyond control. What a way to start a church service. The Holy Spirit does not appear to have read the rubrics. It's hard to imagine in one of our staid congregations, letting ourselves get carried away by such enthusiasm, running the risk of being thought drunk at nine o'clock in the morning.

"What does all this mean?" the people said to each other. The controversy that erupted on the Day of Pentecost and has been raging in the church ever since had to do with the blowing of the Spirit. Where and when does the Spirit blow?

Look at the way the Spirit moved in the early church. It

literally blew the church into existence, gathering a small group of people, ordinary blundering men from out of the world, to become the nucleus of a movement still at work to turn the world upside down. The Spirit cemented together the wayward wills of a cowardly, cowering group of despairing individuals and shot them into a hostile world, as a fellowship of faith, bringing good news of freedom and destiny for the whole world.

It was the Spirit who filled Peter's lungs as he boldly addressed the Sanhedrin. It was the Spirit that helped Stephen look up and see the glory of God and Jesus standing at the right hand, as he died a martyr's death. It was the Spirit who set Paul and Barnabas apart for the mission to the Gentiles. It was the Spirit who took charge of the Council of Jerusalem and its decision to welcome Gentiles into the new community of God and his Christ. It was the Spirit who made an ethnocentric religion into an international missionary apostolate, who raised the sights of the leaders of the church beyond their Jewish particularism to a Christian universalism. The plain truth is that the facts of the gospel became the acts of the Spirit in the ongoing life and mission of the pentecostal community. The church of Jesus Christ is the biography of the Holy Spirit in world history.

Where and when is the Spirit blowing in the church today? For without the primitive Spirit of Pentecost we are way down in the valley of dry bones and the breath we use to chant the liturgy or preach a sermon won't have the power to make them live again. As a pastor you may be renowned as a scholar, a counsellor, an administrator, an activist, an orator, with lots of people to admire the peacock feathers of your pride of achievement, but if you are not simply, in spite of it all, a channel of the Spirit, you will feel hollow, soon burned out, wind-swept, empty scarecrows of accommodation to the relentless pressures of public opinion and the world's relativities around you. Without the Spirit, God is not very near, not here. Without the Spirit, Jesus is a dead hero who lived once upon a time. Without the Spirit, the church is just an organization and your ministry just a job. Without the Spirit, you have no authority, so you must hide behind the so-called authorities and become a manipulator of people. Without the Spirit, the mission becomes church propaganda and bureaucratic wheeling and dealing, not liberating service.

Perhaps with four years of study capped by a theological degree at commencement and sealed by a bishop's hand at ordination, there's nothing to worry about. We've got the Spirit in the bag.

There's an old German story of a young preacher who bragged that he never prepared his sermons. Instead, he trusted the Holy Spirit to put the right words into his mouth. An older man, a veteran preacher, volunteered that the Holy Spirit had spoken to him only once in the pulpit. Once, in the midst of delivering a bad sermon, he heard these words, "Heinrich, you're lazy!"

Talking about the Holy Spirit often makes me nervous. I get nervous because I feel that perhaps we are part of an establishment conspiracy to nail down the Spirit to things we can control. "The wind blows where it wills . . . so it is with everyone who is born of the Spirit." But we want to tie the Spirit down, to make the Spirit come and go as we pull the strings in our ecclesiastical puppet shows. We in the tradition sharing the Spirit of orthodox Christianity can so easily pull the strings of Scripture, bind the Spirit to the canon, enclose him in a creed, wrap him up in the clerical robes of pastor, priest, or bishop, and freeze him in the cold ceremonies of our hand-me-down liturgies. We are the high priests and elders of these esteemed traditions, so at least once a year on the Day of Pentecost, we may have good reason to be skittish about the many ways we imprison the Spirit in our sheltered structures.

And there's another reason to get nervous. That's when we run in the other direction. Tired of the canned spirituality of dead orthodoxy, we try to live on some of our own home-cooked specialties, and let some kind of spirit blow us right off the stage

of real life, out of this matter-of-fact world into some mystical
yonder. It makes me nervous to see Christian leaders and people
imagine they can get in touch with the Spirit by getting in
touch with themselves, by raising their consciousness, by height-
ening their awareness, as though the Holy Spirit who blows
where and when he wills flits along on the wings of one's own
private emotional life, as though the Spirit of Pentecost can be
found in the deep mysteries of Zen, yoga, transcendental meditation, and human potential exercises. The Spirit is not a tele-
pathic medium we can use for our own ends, unless we prefer
to go into the business of being soothsayers, magicians, wizards,
witches, clairvoyants, fortunetellers, and the like. Certainly, we
do not deny such things. There are spiritual powers in the universe, other than the power of the Holy Spirit. The Holy Spirit
is not the only sirocco blowing up a storm in the world. The
tapping of these other elemental energies and the releasing of
these vast subliminal fires are fraught with immense spiritual
danger. "Anyone who does not have the Spirit of Christ," said
Paul, "does not belong to him." The *Didache,* one of the earliest
Christian writings outside the New Testament, warned, "Not
everyone making ecstatic utterances is a prophet, but only the
one who behaves like the Lord."

It does not pay then to jump from the frying pan of orthodoxy, with its externals, into the fires of mysticism, with its inner secrets. We are still caught in that high tension of controversy, asking where and when the Spirit blows in our world
today. That is the question we face in our ministry day after
day. And will we be hung up on a great uncertainty? "Tell me
of your certainties," said Goethe, "I have doubts enough of my
own." Let me tell you some of my certainties—not mine, but
those that come from the One whom Jesus promised the Father
would send in his name, to teach us all things, even the Counsellor, the Paraclete, the Holy Spirit (John 15:25). G. K. Chester-

ton once said, "We've asked all the questions; it's time we started giving some answers."

The first thing is this: Let the Spirit himself be your guide. Do it the Spirit's way! He blows where and when he wills, so what does he will? The Father has spoken his great "Yes!" in his Son Jesus, and his Spirit is out in the world trying to get us to utter "Amen! Hallelujah!" All the Spirit-filled people of the New Testament community did one thing: they witnessed to the Word that had become flesh in Jesus. It's not the noises and sputterings and groans that identify where the Spirit is. The Spirit's way is not to draw attention to himself or to speak on his own authority, but to speak of Christ, to take what belongs to Christ and lift it up in the world. And that's why it's been so difficult to get a clear doctrine of the Holy Spirit in the church, because the Spirit is so self-effacing, and so directing his energies to glorify God the Father and his Son Jesus Christ.

Blowing where and when he wills, doing the Spirit's thing, means radical concentration on the things of Christ, because he is the pioneer of these last days, the revelation of the beginning of the end—the end of all God's ways with his world. So, if you follow the way of the Spirit in your ministry, you will not be skating round the circumference of the faith but will cling instead to the center and magnify his holy name. As Herbert Butterfield put it in one of my favorite quotations: "Stick to Jesus Christ, and as for the rest be totally uncommitted." "Be like the moon," Bishop Ambrose said to his church. You can't be like the sun. Be like the moon, which has no light of its own; and let the Spirit take the light of the sun of God's righteousness and shine upon the face of your ministry, reflecting nothing but that light in the corner of the world which is your mission field.

That's one certainty I feel compelled to leave with you. And a second one is this: Because the Spirit witnesses to the Word, and the Word has become flesh in Jesus, the Spirit has willingly and permanently attached himself to this concrete world. That's why Tillich calls Christianity the religion of the concrete Spirit.

You want to go where the Spirit blows, you want to be ready when the Spirit moves, and you will be bombarded with temptations to take a great spiritual leap out of this world. Many religions, even many Christian groups, think that the Spirit is opposite to matter, the great antithesis to this material, physical, bodily, sensual, earthly realm. It was the wisdom of God that decided that you can't move this world unless you get inside it. That's the incarnational principle. And the Spirit brings the down-to-earth love of God in Jesus even deeper down into the concrete world of ours. There is not a single passage in the Bible that describes the life of the Spirit as anywhere else than here on earth in the human and social body of humanity. In the Spirit heaven has come down to earth.

It was Archimedes who discovered the principle of the lever, that if you place a lever below a mass, you can lift it, and the longer the lever the heavier the mass you can lift. Archimedes said, "Give me a lever long enough, and give me a place outside the world to stand, and I will lift the world." It was from outside the world had to be lifted. Jesus Christ is God's lever from the outside, and the Spirit the power to move that mass.

As one moves about the church, I am prepared to say, with no great opinion polls to back me up, that the greatest failure of preaching and of the church's witness today in general is that it is not enough from above and not enough from below. It is stuck in a bunch of pious piffle and canned religiosity half-way between heaven and earth. Someone has called this an Arianism of the pulpit. You remember the heretic Arius. He believed that Jesus Christ is not fully God and he is not fully human. He is a little less than truly divine and a little less than truly human; he's in a no-man's land half way in-between, making full contact with neither side. So with a lot of preachers who never

quite speak of God and then again never quite reach down deep
into things really human.

We have rarefied the Spirit out of this world of the senses.
That's chiefly our Protestant failing. We do the Holy Spirit of
the Father and Jesus no honor if we elevate him to the realm
of the invisible and untouchable, snatch him away from the
senses like Puritans afraid to see and smell and touch and taste,
as though only the ear—the big ear—is to be filled with the re-
verberations of the Spirit on this earth.

In the Bible the Spirit is not limited to a single sense, to only
one contact with the physical, matter-of-fact world of the senses.
In the Bible the Spirit comes like *fire;* he is called the Spirit of
burning (Isa. 4:4), consuming, purging, enflaming the disciples
with zeal and courage. The Spirit comes like *wind,* animating
dry bones, giving breath and influencing life. The Spirit comes
like pure and fresh *water,* life-giving and refreshing water, in the
regenerating waters of baptism, springing up unto everlasting
life. The Spirit comes like *oil,* anointing those who are sick and
dying with the rich fragrance of healing. The Spirit comes like a
dove, descending from heaven, symbolizing tenderness, inno-
cence, peace and patience. The Spirit takes the flesh of Jesus and
makes it the eucharistic bread of life.

This concrete Spirit of God and his Son Jesus Christ is a
benevolent wind blowing in the midst of world revolutions today, open to the hot winds of discord and the shifting sands of
political passion and economic ferment. Recently I joined a study
seminar travelling in mainland China. We had heard, of course,
the reports about the misery of Christianity under the cultural
revolution. But what came home, as we heard the personal stories
of the surviving martyrs, was an overwhelming sense of the power of the Holy Spirit working in what we had thought was the
modern graveyard of Christianity. During the cultural revolution
every last church in China was shut down, every visible sign of
organized Christianity was destroyed, Bibles were burned, and

leaders were sent down to labor camps. Now, here we found ourselves in the midst of a rebirth of Christian faith and life and
worship in city after city, in houses of worship absolutely
jammed. Fourteen years after the communist government believed it had successfully buried Christianity in the rubble of the
revolution, we found unmistakable evidence in the laboratory
of current world history, that the Holy Spirit is active every-
where, that he blows where and when he wills, that he is the
Spirit of "a god who knew the way out of the grave."

Here we saw Christianity being reborn, stripped down to
basics, no frills, no luxuries, just the facts of the gospel and the
acts of the Spirit. This involves faith, a charismatic fellowship
gathered around the Word, sighs of freedom and tears of joy
in the wake of incredible suffering, and a radiant hope for the
future, for a whole new world, in spite of the staggering odds
which any intelligence can compute. There we experienced a
real bond of fellowship in the Spirit who proceeds eternally from
the Father and the Son, across the otherwise insurmountable
barriers of culture, language, color, nationality, ideology, and
also food and drink and everything else that counts for real
among human beings. There, if ever anywhere one's soul needed
proof positive of the Spirit alive in the world, there is a humanity groaning with the birth pangs of the kingdom. There is the
risen Christ alive in the worship, there is the gospel the power
of life, there is the church alive in the Word, there is a New
Pentecost in the liturgy of memorial and anticipation; there is
the witness to the crucified Jesus in the sufferings of the martyrs.
Let us give thanks to God for the Spirit who is still being poured
out upon all flesh, so that whoever calls upon the name of the
Lord will be saved.

Part Two
SPECIAL OCCASIONS

God's Own Most Personal Act

When we were children, we were slaves to the elemental spirits of the universe. But when the time had fully come, God sent forth his Son, born of a woman, born under the law, to redeem those who were under the law, so that we might receive adoption as sons. And because you are sons, God has sent the Spirit of his Son into our hearts, crying "Abba! Father!" So through God you are no longer a slave but a son, and if a son then an heir.

Formerly, when you did not know God, you were in bondage to beings that by nature are no gods; but now that you have come to know God, or rather to be known by God, how can you turn back again to the weak and beggarly elemental spirits, whose slaves you want to be once more? You observe days, and months, and seasons, and years! I am afraid I have labored over you in vain.
—GALATIANS 4:3-11

Once a year we set aside a day to celebrate the Reformation of the church in the 16th century. We also call upon God for many returns of the Spirit of reform to continue the work of Martin Luther in our time. We concentrate on the center of our own

81

tradition, and ask about the roots of our own Lutheran identity. The Lutheran element in our makeup goes back to a theological professor. In 1517 Martin Luther took a hammer and nailed his 95 theses to the door of the Wittenberg church, to announce his protest against the sale of forgiveness for money, quite apart from faith and repentance. "Once the coin in the coffer rings, the soul from purgatory springs."

Luther once made a startling statement: "My gospel has nothing to do with the things of this world. It is something unique, exclusively concerned with souls. To promote and settle the affairs of the temporal life is not a duty of my office, but of those called to this work, the emperor, the nobility, and the magistrates. And the source upon which they must draw is not the gospel, but reason, tradition, and equity."

The gospel is something unique; it is God's own most personal act. One verse in Galatians says, "God sent forth his Son, born of a woman, born under the law." There can be no more personal act of a Father than the sending of his Son on a mission to a far off country. The purpose of this trip is also clear. While we were slaves to the elemental spirits of the universe, we have been liberated from that bondage. We have become adopted as children of God, and so we can say in our hearts, "Abba! Father!", and we can call the Son who was sent to our country our very own brother, our liberator, our friend.

There have been countless sermons preached on the Reformation during the last four centuries. I looked into my own file of sermons on the Reformation, and I also contemplated the many sermons I have heard and read over the years. They all fall into three different piles; they all deal with three different types of crises. I could see one stack of sermons dealing with the *crisis of conscience*. These sermons focused on the struggle going on deep inside each one of us as individual persons. In theology we call it the existentialist factor in Luther's Reformation. There was Luther ripped apart by anxiety, full of dread, fear, doubt and

scared to death of death itself. So he entered a monastery. Today
he would have been sent to a psychiatrist and he would have
been put on drugs to calm the screaming voice of conscience
within. But he went to a monastery to work out his problems.
He didn't use psychological language. Rather, he thought in
terms of working out his own salvation. But everything he tried
failed to help his anxiety-ridden conscience. He read the Bible;
it made matters worse. There's a lot of bad news in the Bible.
He received the sacraments but he remained in hellish torment.
He did everything his church superiors told him, but he could
find no release from the inner suffering.

Then it suddenly broke loose for him. In letters of Paul to the
Galatians and Romans he got hold of the good news of God's
own most personal act in Jesus Christ, and he grasped it with
an absolute faith. As long as Luther lived under the law of God
and the demands of his conscience, he remained in the realm of
degrees, of more or less, partial success and clever compromise.
But nothing less than an absolute faith in the gospel could bring
the final peace for the conscience terrified by sin, despair, and
death. That's a brief sketch of Luther in the throes of the conscience crisis, Luther the existentialist, as we would say today.
He found in the gospel the power of absolute salvation, based on
God's most personal act in Jesus Christ.

I saw, in the second place, another stack of sermons dealing
with the *crisis in the church*. These sermons dealt with the tragic
split in the church, dividing Christendom into churches fighting
each other. In these sermons we look at Luther, the pioneering
reformer of a church he loved enough to fight against all its
corruption. There had been other critics of the church, notably
Erasmus, the humanist of Rotterdam. But for Luther all these
other critics measured the church by something less than the
gospel. A true reformation must come from the gospel and deal
with the heart of the church, not by treating the symptoms with
a few aspirins of reform.

Until a few months ago we lived in Flossmoor, a beautiful suburb. Lots of evergreens were growing on our huge lot, but some of them looked like they were dying. The branches were drying, starting from below. So I called the tree doctor. He told me that we could only revive the tree by nourishing the roots. Cutting off the dead branches will make the tree look better for awhile, but that won't make the tree get well. It's more than a matter of pruning the branches. The renewal of the church is more a question of restructuring the church and all that. We must get down to the roots of the church with the healing power of the gospel. Luther found it; he found it in God's own most personal act in Jesus Christ, and only the power of His Word could scour the church of all its corruption. This was the same Word that gave him an absolute faith for a crisis in conscience.

If we are looking for a renewal of the church, for a recovery of its lost unity, and for a rebirth of vision and mission, then the way is not to become more ecumenical-than-thou but to find all these things as an echo, a reflex action, of God's own most personal gift to the church in Jesus Christ. The road to reformation goes through the heart of the gospel into the arteries and veins of the church body. And in no other way.

Finally, there is a third type of sermon, and this has to do with the *crisis of culture*. Examples of this type of sermon I could hardly find in my own stack of sermons and what I did find was very bad. I suppose it's easier to identify with the struggle of conscience. We experience it immediately. It's also easier to identify with the call to reform the church. We're all experts in criticizing the church, with a hodge-podge of ideas from Luther and Kierkegaard, or Marx and Freud, or lesser lights like Berger and Cox.

But the gospel of God's own most personal act in Jesus Christ speaks also to the crisis of culture. It's not only the conscience, not only the church, but the whole of culture that is addressed by the sending of God's Son into the world. It's in this culture, this concrete worldly context in all its dimensions, that we find ourselves slaves to the elemental spirits of the universe. What are the elemental spirits of the universe? They are the beings that are by nature no gods—the fashions, the myths, the ideologies, the laws, the religions—all the old and new soteriologies to which we and our people are slaves.

History is one of them. Millions of modern people are trapped in the belief that history will save them. In getting rid of the God of history, they have only history itself to carry the load of their salvation. So this secular history turns a trick and becomes the sacred thing. Hence, Marxists have a greater confidence in the miracles history will perform than even primitive people expected from their deities. So history, which is no god at all, has to become capitalized and spoken of in great reverential tones. "I am warning you," said Nikita Khrushchev to Abdel Nasser in 1961, "I am warning you in all seriousness. I tell you that communism is sacred." Of course, it has to be sacred, because it supposedly holds the master key to the dialectics of history that promise the salvation of mankind.

Science is another of the elemental spirits of the universe. For millions of us it carries the hope of our deliverance. So we have to capitalize Science, and what we capitalize in our belief system becomes our God. We look to it for help in every time of need. We believe it has the answers, if only we'll tithe our resources for the sake of more research. It's the only respectable language, so even the nonsense of a Von Daniken about beings from outer space has to be clothed in scientific language to create the optical illusion that it's something more than a mixture of superstition and fiction.

Here too it's God's own most personal act in Jesus Christ that frees us to keep our science beneath the cross of salvation and free from the pretension of a substitute God.

When we look around we can see the faces of these elemental spirits peering out all over. Some of these faces are painted like the whores of religion. More people read the daily horoscope than any other part of the newspaper, the polls tell us. If medals of the Virgin and St. Christopher won't do, then there are medals with all the signs of the zodiac, and they have been found to work just as well. There is a religious connection also, I think, with the fascination of films about the devil, vampires, and magic. Millions of people are attracted to all this stuff, and to them Rosemary's Baby is more exciting than the gospel according to St. Paul.

So *Religion* is one of the elemental spirits. Take any of our modern secular cities, and you'll find religion breaking through the concrete and glass and plastic surfaces. People with problems are patronizing thousands of soothsayers, spiritualists, and fortunetellers. People are buying amulets, good luck charms and Hindu goddesses, more than Luther's parishioners ever purchased their certificates of indulgence. They'll pay anything and commit any folly to enter into the mysterious, to have an exotic experience or to control their uncertain future through astrology, palmistry or talismans. At the core of our modern advanced, secular, scientific, technological society there are demons of religion that have not been swept away.

What I am saying is that we must broaden the theme of the Reformation to encompass the horizon of the entire culture in which the crises of conscience and church take place. We have a slogan in our tradition which in Latin goes: *ecclesia semper reformanda*—the church must always be reformed. We also say, the Reformation must go on. It must go on in the name of God's own most personal act in Jesus Christ. But we must no longer confine it to the sphere of personal conscience; we must no longer make it an intramural game between the churches. We must carry the battle to the world. We must translate the church into a liberation of the world in the power of God's own most personal act in Jesus Christ.

We have mentioned only History, Science and Religion as

"spirits of the world" which carry the load of modern salvation, which we therefore capitalize and divinize and ritualize. But we could go on and on for the elemental spirits are legion. Think of how the good life is exalted in materialistic terms, in terms of the vicious cycle of production, advertising and consumption. Ours is a consumer society. The restlessness in the world between the first and second and third worlds is a mad furious competition to quench an infinite thirst for more consumer goods. That has become the meaning of life, the locus of the sacred, the ultimate mystery before which we prostrate ourselves. "Modern man", says Jacques Ellul, "places his hope, his faith, his assurance, his happiness, his security, and the development of his personality in the use and possession of more and more technical objects". They have become the substitutes for religion in a technological society.

One other world-enthralling spirit is Politics. Politics has become the new shape of religion in the world. In Luther's day people somehow poured their religious energies and loyalties into their churches. Then came the religious wars, the Enlightenment and the resulting secularization of the modern states. What happened was that vast numbers of people transferred their religious hopes and commitments from the church to secular politics. Politics became their religion. Political ideology has become the modern substitute for dogmatic theology.

Political religion is marked by the cult of personality. The dictator's will becomes the personal power at the heart of the universe. Absolute loyalty is demanded; no heresy is tolerated. The mark of religion is total faith. The political party has taken the place of the church. The ideologues are the theologians and the commissars are the clergy applying the dogma in every cell.

How can there be freedom within the growing web of totalitarianism? Where is the point of support when history, science, religion, economics and politics make total claims on us, when they become like gods? The point of the Reformation today, its relevance for us, is the clear witness to God's own most personal act in Jesus Christ. Here is where the message comes to grips with the crisis of our culture. Here faith becomes free from false substitutes for God. Here the church is kept from bowing to the gods of this world and conspiring with them to hold the conscience of people in bondage. Here by looking to the face of God in Jesus Christ we can withstand the seductions of the elemental spirits of the universe.

I began by qouting Martin Luther. I would like to close by revising his statement. When he said, "My gospel has nothing to do with the things of this world. It is something unique, exclusively concerned with souls," I would say, "Yes, indeed, the gospel is something unique. But it has everything to do with the things of this world. It keeps the things from becoming the gods of this world. It keeps them in their place. It keeps the things of the world from becoming the hope of our salvation. It keeps the world worldly, it keeps history, science, religion and business and politics from becoming absolute, totalitarian, and the objects of human trust."

The Earth Is the Lord's!

The earth is the Lord's and the fulness thereof, the world and those who dwell therein.
                                    —PSALM 24:1

The earth is the Lord's. It's time to give thanks. The earth is the Lord's. It doesn't belong to us. We are guests! So why do we pollute and destroy our planetary home? We are all in the same boat of creation. We have been created together with all the creatures of the earth.

The mystical tradition placed the highest premium on God and the soul. The biblical Christian tradition puts the accent on God and the body, God in the body of our earthly humanity. The earth is the Lord's and the fulness thereof. So why are we sending the earth to the gas chamber?

The earth is the Lord's, the fulness thereof. So why do we treat it like so much dead matter, to do with as we please? Why do we gouge the earth for its raw materials, pouring these divine blessings into the bottomless pits of our greedy stomachs?

The earth is the Lord's and the fulness thereof. So why are we now going to create more megatons of explosives, to develop the potential to ruin the land and the seas and threaten the whole human race?

The earth is the Lord's and the fulness thereof. It's good for us to remember that the promise of salvation includes the earth. We together with the earth have a common destiny in the kingdom of God. The covenant of God includes the whole earth. Even the cosmos that Carl Sagan talks about belongs to the Lord, and when he talks about millions and millions of years, you realize that we human beings are recent newcomers on one of the younger planets in the universe.

The entire span of human and cosmic life is moving within the orbit of God's plan for the whole creation . . . not just for us individual persons, and not just for humanity as a whole, but, if you believe the promises of God, you will include in your cosmic vision the stars and the planets, the winds and the waves, the rocks and the rivers, and everything that moves on the land and swims in the sea.

It's very narrow for us to reduce the biblical vision of God to the human scene of life and history going on for only a millenium or two. The earth has a glory and a beauty wonderful to behold. In its own way it has something to tell us of the glory of God.

But the other side of the coin is tragedy. The world of nature seems to have a share in the human tragedy, existing in a state of bondage, groaning under a tyranny that will not release it to its full potential in the kingdom of God. So meanwhile we are intertwined with the fate of this earth, with its floods and fires, tornadoes, blizzards, hurricanes, hailstorms, earthquakes, volcanoes, pests, plagues, and famines. No wonder that human beings have gotten the notion that we are in a fierce competition with nature, our environment. We seem to live under a curse, ekeing out a precarious existence in toilsome drudgery and bloody sweat.

Some religions teach the way of escape out of this inhospitable world. Our hope of salvation lies in the down-to-earth coming of the Messiah, who brings a word of peace for the whole world of human life and our earthly home. Can it be that, "The wolf will dwell with the lamb, and the leopard lie down with the kid"? The earth is the Lord's and the future thereof. Will there be a time of harmony between humans and animals, a time for the renewal of all things the Lord has made? It is written, "Even the winds and the waves obey him," the Lord of the universe.

The reign of death in the cosmos has been broken. Thanksgiving is the eucharist of the new creation in Jesus Christ and the sanctification of the natural, breathing the life of resurrection into the body of this life, through the elements of the earth which we eat and which we drink. Eating and drinking are the events in our life which link the most physical things we do to the most central symbols of God's gifts of life and salvation. These symbols are not mere metaphors or empty signs. They are filled with the coming of God into his creation and our creaturely life, to bring his redemption deep into our bodies and our souls.

The Living Temple

Do you not know that your body is a temple of the Holy Spirit within you, which you have from God? You are not your own; you were bought with a price. So glorify God in your body.
                                    —1 CORINTHIANS 6:19-20

Like many of you, I'm sure, I grew up in the bosom of the church. I heard its lengthy sermons, listened to its solemn prayers, learned its Sunday School lessons, sang its hymns, attended its parochial schools, and all of my teaching years have been in a seminary. The total impression could so easily lead to the conclusion that a person is made up of two parts, the body and the soul, and that while there exists a specialist in town for every part of the body, even the most unmentionable ones, Christianity has a monopoly on the soul. "God and the soul," St. Augustine said, "I would know only God and the soul."

It's a long story, involving theological study and personal experience, about how I came to the belief that Christianity may be the truest religion, but it's lost half of its biblical wits. It's lost a large part of the truth. It fell victim along the way to a creeping spiritualism. The story of the Bible tells about how God created people from the stuff of the earth, and breathed life into the body. It tells about how God entered this world in the flesh and blood of a Jew.

Plato was the greatest of the philosophers from Greece. He had the idea that the "true philosopher is entirely concerned with the soul and not the body." When Christianity came along, a few hundred years later, the world was swirling with Plato's religion of the soul, trying to release the soul from the chains of the body, and rising upwards into the empyrean of a purely spiritual heaven for eternal life with God in the soul.

Now believe it or not, the garden-variety Christianity in both the pulpits and the pews has peddled a good deal of Plato's idealistic philosophy of the soul, even while intending to preach nothing but the gospel truth of the Bible. It's a long story, how the Greek idea of the salvation of souls became more attractive to Christians than the Hebrew idea of the salvation of the whole person, which includes the body.

Many Christians have become obsessed with their souls and neglected their bodies—as if we can ever have one without the other. As if we can save the soul without the body, as if God would have created our body as a prison-house of the soul, as a dungeon which we have to leave in order to fly into some ethereal realm of weightless, shapeless, and literally sense-less souls.

Paul says, in effect, don't you know that your body is the temple of the Spirit? Don't you know that God has taken up residence in the human body, and that you will come to glorify God in your body or not at all? St. Paul must have feared that Christians were losing the good news of God meeting us in the flesh . . . the good news of the incarnation. The Word is embodied in flesh. God is in the human body, the body of Jesus, the risen body of Christ. The body and blood of our Lord meets us in the bread we break and the wine we drink. Christianity is a religion of the body. But look what has happened—the very thing that St. Paul feared. Christians would forget to glorify God in their bodies. Instead, all that asceticism, gnosticism, spiritualism, puritanism, escapism, mysticism, treating the body as the source of sin and the root of all evil. That's to commit treason against the body and to hanker for mystical life with God in some immaterial realm where ghosts or angels but not real solid people feel at home.

We know that the body is beautiful because God made it. We also know that our bodies have been invaded by sin and suffering and death. The same St. Paul cried, "Who can deliver me from this body of death?" But your body itself is not the source of all that is rotten in you. When you are tempted to give your body the blame, when you feel like the body is filthy, like a bag of worms, remember this, your *body* is for the Lord; God made it. It is the temple of the Spirit; the tabernacle of Christ, the framework of meaning in the person you are. In Christian faith the body and soul go together. The soul is the meaning of the body, and the body is the organic system in which it negotiates God's meaning in human life. They are the inner and outer dimensions of the one indivisible psychosomatic unity of the whole person.

But what is happening today? The old split that came in with Hellenistic religion is happening today. Religion is taking hold of the soul again. There is a religious revival in the land. One sign of it you can see at almost any airport. These kids with their Krishna consciousness are trying to turn people on to some kind of transcendental spirituality. Christianity is the complete opposite of transcendentalizing the soul. It is a down-to-earth faith in the incarnation of God in history, in our body, in our vital material world of day-to-day existence. Many Christians are back into the old-time religion of separating the soul from the body, of cutting ties with the natural life of real people on earth. There is a trend in Christianity to rummage around inside for a thing called the soul and to turn its gaze to some inner world of spirituality far removed from the kingdom-power which Jesus brought down to earth, in a form we can grasp right here and now in our bodies and our life together.

That's one trend. And the other is that the body becomes secularized. Separated from the soul, it becomes a toy or plaything to do with as we please. Paul says, "The body is for the Lord." We have lost touch with our secularized bodies. Far from being the temple of the Spirit, they have become the dumping grounds of chemicals and pollutants which do nothing for health but make us sick. We have become strangers to our bodies . . . pooped out, broken down, out of breath, out of shape, over-weight, undernourished, drugged, victims of surgery. Most Americans have bodies with missing parts, a condition we would hardly tolerate of our automobiles—a missing headlight, a missing gear, a missing air filter, a missing muffler, even a missing rear-end. Never in the history of mankind has the human body become so mangled, so incomplete.

I believe that Christianity is called today to hold up the dignity of the body and to fight for its integrity on every front. One of the most heinous crimes which the Nazis committed against the Jews was to desecrate their temples. Modern secular culture is committing crimes against the temple of the Spirit. Our bodies have a right to clean air and pure water. But some people think they have a right to pollute these things, if only it can make them richer. As though the private right to make money is a higher right than the peoples' right to have the things of nature as clean and as good for the body as the Lord of Creation gave to his creatures in the first place.

We have only begun to reclaim the biblical message that God has come and is still coming down to earth, in human bodies and amidst earthly things that we can touch with our hands and see with our eyes. This ties the holiness of God to the health of our flesh and blood, our skin and hair, hands and feet, lungs and stomach and all that we need from the natural world to make human life more beautiful, the very living temple of God's presence in the world.

The test of a vital Christianity today is whether it claims the whole person, the whole of life for Christ's sake, the Redeemer of our body, linking faith to the body of mankind and the elements of the earth. What this can mean for the ecology movement, we have only begun to realize. What it means for the way we produce and distribute foods for people, we have only begun to ask. What it means for health care, for the way we care for the sick and aging in this society, we have barely begun to explore. How can we make our Christian schools and congregations institutes for the life and health of the whole person, and not merely retreats in which we try to make pious people more pious and good people a little bit better? For Christianity, if it is true to its birthright, brings meaning and wholeness to our common life in the body, in all its personal, social, and earthly dimensions.

The Politics of God

What causes wars, and what causes fightings among you? Is it not your passions that are at war in your members? You desire and do not have; so you kill. And you covet and cannot obtain; so you fight and wage war. You do not have, because you do not ask. You ask and do not receive, because you ask wrongly, to spend it on your passions. Unfaithful creatures! Do you not know that friendship with the world is enmity with God? Therefore whoever wishes to be a friend of the world makes himself an enemy of God. Or do you suppose it is in vain that the scripture says, "He yearns jealously over the spirit which he has made to dwell in us"? But he gives more grace; therefore it says, "God opposes the proud, but gives grace to the humble." Submit yourselves therefore to God. Resist the devil and he will flee from you. Draw near to God and he will draw near to you. Cleanse your hands, you sinners, and purify your hearts, you men of double mind. Be wretched and mourn and weep. Let your laughter be turned to

*mourning and your joy to dejection. Humble yourselves
before the Lord and he will exalt you.*
—JAMES 4:1-10

This day is appointed as the commemoration of the bishop of
Oslo during the Second World War . . . Bishop Eivind Berggrav.
He was the strong leader of the fight waged by the Norwegian
Church against Naziism, the Bonhoeffer of Norway, imprisoned
by the Quisling puppet-government for three years for his role
in the struggle of the church against a demonic state. He was the
author of a document similar to the Barmen Declaration. He
once said, "Have you noticed how full of life the Bible has become, as if written for people in war and during times of occu-
pation." As Quisling's men took him by car to his prison, he
took out his New Testament and read from 1 Peter, "Have no
fear of them, nor be troubled, but in your hearts reverence Christ
as Lord." The bishop's declaration, called the "Foundation of the
Church," was read in all the churches on Easter Day. Like the
Barmen Declaration, it contained a simple basic confession of
Jesus Christ as Lord, the Lord of human life in all its dimensions.

Bishop Berggrav observed that Christians have learned quite
easily to accept Jesus Christ as their personal Savior, because then
they can confine him to their spiritual life, the realm of religion.
But they cannot accept him as Lord, because then that brings
his lordship into the midst of life in all its aspects, permitting no
sphere of life to buckle under to the totalitarian ideologies and
their puffed-up leaders: "God opposes the proud, but gives grace
to the humble."

Berggrav was kept in solitary confinement, where like Bonhoeffer he wrote letters and papers, made friends with his guards,
who, incidentally, were ordered not even to talk to the bishop,
because word was leaked to Quisling that the prisoner was con-
verting his guards. According to Quisling's plan, the bishop was
to be shot after a hasty trial, as an impostor and traitor, but

Himmler and his Nazis overruled it for their own reasons, prob-
ably so as not to stir up the people anymore.

We remember witnesses like Bonhoeffer and Berggrav, not because they were national heroes and their struggles dramatic.
But they were witnesses to the politics of the biblical God. The
axiom of the politics of God is this: He opposes the proud, but
gives grace to the humble. These men—Bonhoeffer, Niemöller,
Berggrav—are witnesses to the truth, that the judgment of God
is at work in history, not only in Israel but among the nations,
not only in the Christian soul but in the world of war and
politics. Isaiah said, "The Lord is a God of justice."

It is a notoriously dangerous thing to preach the politics of
God. You have had the flattering experience, some of you, perhaps, that when you preach a pious sermon on Jesus as Savior
from sin and guilt, people may weep and warmly pump your
hand after church. But if you preach a political sermon, the
politics of God and Jesus as Lord, you may not feel the people's
warmth, but a chill to make you think twice next time.

After the war Berggrav became a famous world churchman
and ecumenical leader. His book, *Man and State,* was widely
read and its ideas debated. He strongly attacked the traditional
Lutheran stance of obedience to governmental authority. He
called for Christian resistance to the demonic trends in the
modern totalitarian states, threatening all decent human life.
After the War, some strict Lutherans attacked his ideas, on the
grounds they violated the Two Kingdoms doctrine as German
Lutheranism had understood it.

But Berggrav knew his Bible. The prophetic tradition always
meddled in the politics of the time, and so did Luther. Berggrav
stated: "Lately we are often asked to consider what Luther has
to say about the two realms. It is time to set the matter straight:
To Luther as to us there is only one realm, the realm of God."

It is so crucial for us to examine and recapture this political
motif of the Bible, because our preaching about warm fuzzy

feelings has turned out to be good for nothing. The prophets who preached the politics of God were not meddling liberals, cranky conservatives, or insurgent radicals. They did not opt for one of the parties, one of the going isms. But they didn't do nothing either. They were not quietists.

The judgment of God is at work in a strange way, in that paradoxical power to reverse the usual order of things in our experience. The first will be last, and the last will be first. Sinners enter into the kingdom of God before the righteous ones; the greatest among you is the servant of others. The exalted ones are an abomination to God; the lowly ones will be up front. The proud will be put down; the unimportant folk will be lifted up. That is the strange politics of God in the rough and tumble of history!

After the war Bishop Berggrav had to temper the cry for vengeance against the Quislings that had been raised all over the country. People wanted revenge. It's an eye for an eye and a tooth for a tooth. The bishop was attacked for being too mild; "a silken bishop," they called him, for his silly notion of trying to win the guilty ones back into society, proposing an extensive access to mercy. Berggrav even called for mercy for Quisling. Unbelievable. It's time for revenge! for getting the upper hand! But Berggrav said, "It's time to forgive and to forget. For every evil deed that has been done, we must work a deed of mercy; otherwise the wheel of cruelty will roll on."

The gospel at last was at work. The gross and despicable deeds of the powerful people of history are evils that have roots in each one of us. These roots of evil can be traced to the depths of all of us, the rich and the poor, the mighty and the lowly, the winners and the losers. In the politics of God, this politics of a transcendent dimension, we are all part of the same lump of humanity. The same roots of evil are to be found in all of us. We are called to repentance and therefore to be generous in compassion for those who now stand accused and condemned.

After the Civil War, Abraham Lincoln exhibited this same stroke of humble compassion: "Both sides, North and South," he cried, "read the same Bible and pray to the same God." There's no health in gloating over victory. That will only start the whole game of pride and arrogance over again. Pride is the root of all evil. It began that way in the Garden; Paradise Lost! But judgment paves the way for cleansing, repentance, compassion, reconciliation, and new hope for human politics free of dirty deals, beyond power-politics, beyond divide and conquer, beyond search and destroy, beyond decadence and death, beyond graft and greed. Bishop Berggrav had his mind trained to understand the biblical politics of God, so he was the man God could use in the critical hours of his church and his people. God grant that we may be possessed of the same Spirit of courage and wisdom and understanding today.

Who Is Jesus Christ for Us Today?

Now when Jesus came into the district of Caesarea Philippi, he asked his disciples, "Who do men say that the Son of man is?" And they said, "Some say John the Baptist, others say Elijah, and others Jeremiah or one of the prophets." He said to them, "But who do you say that I am?" Simon Peter replied "You are the Christ, the Son of the living God." And Jesus answered him, "Blessed are you, Simon Bar-Jona! For flesh and blood has not revealed this to you, but my Father who is in heaven."

—MATTHEW 16:13-17

The twentieth century is still grappling with the question Jesus addressed to his disciples at Caesarea Philippi: "Who do you say that I am?" It still strikes us with its original enigmatic force. Even many people who do not believe Jesus is the Christ, the Son of the living God, have a high regard for his teachings and try to practice them.

The story of the search for the real Jesus of history coincides with the breakup of classical orthodoxy and the beginning of

102

modern Protestant theology. The land in which this search has bloomed, withered and revived again and again is Germany. One of the truly exciting chapters in modern biblical scholarship has been the attempt to lay hold of the historical Jesus, as he really was, and then to figure out his true meaning for humanity and history. Since the eighteenth century, not only believers but scholars have been busy answering the question Jesus put at Caesarea Philippi: "Who do people say that I am?"

For over a millenium and a half the church had fixed an answer to this question in the ancient creeds and councils of the church. We still recite the old answers of the church in the Apostles' Creed and the Nicene Creed, which build on Peter's confession. "We believe in one Lord Jesus Christ, the only Son of God, eternally begotten of the Father, God from God." And these confessions affirm the true divinity and true humanity of Jesus Christ.

But then in the eighteenth century these creedal and confessional bandages were removed from the historical figure of Jesus. The old dogmas of the church were suspended or bracketed out. Scholars wanted to know the actual personality of the historical Jesus, the flesh-and-blood vitality of the real man, not merely what his followers believed and taught about him. Biographers relish the thought of writing about the great figures of history. Artists and dramatists have been challenged to practice their skills on Jesus of Nazareth. Albert Schweitzer wrote what is now a classic on the modern *Quest of the Historical Jesus*. What he showed is that all the biographers failed. They all painted a picture of Jesus as a fulfillment of their own wish, as a projection of their own ideals. Behind the mass of scholarly details we can see the image of each scholar superimposed on his portrayal of Jesus. Like plastic surgeons making over the face of the patient in their own image, or perhaps like artists who paint themselves into the figures they create, the modern biographical and psychological presentations have built in modern ideas and modern values. They have all succumbed to what Henry Cadbury of Harvard University called, "The Peril of Modernizing Jesus."

Look at the pile of pictures we have in the albums of modern critical scholarship. Jesus looks like an effete romanticist in Ernst Renan, like a rationalistic deist in Heinrich Paulus, as a God-intoxicated mystic in Friedrich Schleiermacher, as a pure mythic hero in Bruno Bauer, as an apocalyptic fanatic in Albert Schweitzer, as a socialist reformer among the Marxists, and as we turn the pages we come to the contemporary section where we find Jesus looking like an existentialist philosopher, like the founder of the institute on positive mental attitude, like a guerrilla fighter overthrowing the ruling class, like the leader of the black power movement, etc. You're tempted to conclude that Jesus is treated as so much putty in the hands of the clever people, who want to use him as a tool of their own schemes and interests.

So, who is Jesus Christ, really? And how can we know for sure? What difference does it make, anyway? What's riding on it for us?

Now, it may be that this weird collection of pictures of Jesus in the galleries of modern scholarship has something to say to us about the real nature of the person of Jesus. The very pluralism we face may tell us that Jesus is not easy to understand. It may not be our fault, due to our stubborn wills and narrow minds, that we cannot capture a credible image that we can all accept. This pluralism may point to the enigma, to the "mystery," to use an old word, of the person of Jesus himself, making it appear that he has many faces, depending on what angle you choose to look from. It may be that his many dimensions account for the fact that he eludes the clutch of our categories, and transcends all our available analogies, even though he is a human being. He is a man, a human being, a part of our history, sharing fully our kind of time and experience. He is very much like all of us. Yet, he is different. The Creed says that he is so different, that only the biggest little word in our vocabulary can finally capture the category difference, the word "God." He is truly human, like the rest of us; he is also very God, and that puts him in a class of his own. So he is called the only-begotten, the one and only Savior, the one and only Lord, the one and only Messiah, the one and only liberator. There is a long list of titles applied to Jesus, each bringing out one facet of his total being and meaning.

The collection of writings called the New Testament contains virtually all the knowledge we possess about this Jesus of Nazareth, the Christ, the Son of the living God. All of this knowledge comes to us in the form of witness. There is no purely objective historical knowledge about this man, untouched by the energies of faith and witness. In this little book, we can see no non-christological picture of the historical Jesus. Only believers in Christ have told us what it means to be followers of Jesus . . . so much so that we actually conflate the two terms, and simply say Jesus Christ, as though Christ were not a title, but the second name of Jesus.

And we have not only one title, but many. If we should try to strip away all the titles, and then ask the real Jesus of history to stand up, nobody would respond. Nobody would answer to the name "Jesus," apart from the titles that distinguish his identity and memory in world history. There is no Jesus who is merely Jesus. The scholars haven't found anything like that, and they have tried very hard. When all the titles have been laid aside, as a critical experiment, some scholars have hypothesized there's nothing left. It's like peeling an onion; there is no seed inside. It's all peeling. So perhaps Jesus never even existed? Many books, long learned books, have been written to prove that Jesus of Nazareth never existed. He's supposedly just the creation of people who wanted to quit fishing, run a congregation, and make an easy living.

Now let us take a flying jump into the 16th century. Melanchthon, Luther's right hand man, said, "To know Christ is to know his benefits." I think it still stands as a sage statement on this

side of the mountain of modern critical scholarship. The New
Testament abounds with titles which serve to identify the uniqueness of Jesus. We're not so sure what the historical Jesus thought
about himself. He did not run around like Muhammad Ali,
bragging about how great he is; he did not say he was Jesus
Christ Superstar. He asked questions. He did not give the answer, except the answer of his life and actions. Actions speak
louder than words. So it was with Jesus. But the New Testament
gives lots of answers. They are the answers of the followers of
Jesus and believers in him as the Christ.

There is a bias for sure in the apostolic witness to Jesus, the
Christ of the living God. It's the bias of faith. To use the word
of the language-analysis theologians, there is an apostolic "blik"
at work in the earliest preaching and witness to Jesus, and this
"blik" is written into all the documents we possess which give
us any clue at all about Jesus. They talk about Jesus as the
Christ, the Son of God, Lord, Savior, Logos, High Priest, Servant of God, Prophet . . . and many others. These titles were
conferred upon Jesus in the light of faith and the experience of
the risen presence of the living Jesus. These are titles which at-
tribute to Jesus the functions of divinity. Jesus is the Savior, but
isn't it true that only God can save? Jesus is the Lord, but isn't
it true that only God is the Lord of lords? Jesus is the Logos—
the Word—but isn't it true that the Word was with God and
the Word was God? Isn't Jesus the subject of names which are
above all other names, because they bespeak the work which only
God can do? They speak eloquently of the uniqueness of Jesus.
He is not only the founder of Christianity; nay, more than that,
he is the *foundation* of the salvation which God has in store
for the whole of humanity.

So, if you ask me, "Who is this Christ who redeems?" I
could hand you a fish, and you would know the answer. One of
the earliest symbols of Christianity was the fish. In Greek the

letters that spelled fish—IXTHUS—represented an ancient chris-
tological confession: Jesus Christ Son of God Savior.

If a person asks you for a fish, will you give him a serpent?
(Matt. 7:10). If you're rummaging around in the wastebaskets
of the past, looking for some Jesus, minus the names and titles
and symbols that speak of his unique saving meaning, you'll get
a serpent, but not a fish.

Does that mean that our Christian faith is built on nothing but
a fish story? Does the primitive Christian claim seem fishy to
us today, that this Jesus, the man from Nazareth, crucified under
Pontius Pilate, just outside the gate among the terrorists and
criminals, is today the living Messiah, the risen Lord, and the
final Savior of the world? Were they not stretching things a
bit much, those men and women who left the tomb on Easter
morning, huddled in a house on Pentecost, and then virtually
sprang upon the world with the good news of the gospel of salvation through Jesus the Christ, going forth from Jerusalem, and
from Judea, and to the far ends of the earth, so that even we
can say that we have heard the same message and really believe
the very same gospel?

He Who Hears You Hears Me!

He who hears you hears me, and he who rejects you rejects me, and he who rejects me rejects him who sent me.
—LUKE 10:16

We live in a culture that is hard of hearing. True, we have hearing aids. We have libraries, more books and magazines, more Ph.D's and experts, more tools and techniques to help us get the Gospel message through. But still, ours is a culture that is hard of hearing. There are a number of reasons.

First, there is the problem of boredom with language. If every day we are being buried under an avalanche of words, we settle down to twenty minutes of holy monotony when the sermon comes on. The late German thinker, Martin Heidegger, lamented the mass production of counterfeit words by which all the great institutions of culture do their business. The politicians, the mass media, the industrial complex, and the churches specialize in words, but with less and less public trust. Words like "credibility gap" and "cover-up" are a new indication that people become very suspicious of the great word makers of our culture.

109

Second, people feel that words are impotent. Actions, not words. Practice, not theory, will save us. Many of the restless people who struggle for justice and freedom agree with Karl Marx that so far we have only given people different religious or philosophical interpretations of the world; but the point is to change it so that it comes closer to the messianic hope which Marxism holds out. Here, too, people are not inclined to expect that the words and symbols and sacraments of the Christian faith will do much to change the stubborn and bitter realities of our experience.

Third, words are deceptive, being used to cover up the very reality they were meant to reveal. Words give sanction to the status quo, provide a kind of sanctimonious benediction on the existing situation. Too often the priest and functionary of religion conspire with special interest groups to deceive people and keep them under control.

Be all that as it may, we need to be reminded that no matter how poisoned the language systems become, no matter how deaf the culture is, there is no future for the faith apart from the living Word. "How are people to call upon him in whom they have not believed? And how are they to believe in him of whom they have never heard? And how are they to hear without a preacher?" (Rom. 10:14-15).

The Word preached, heard, and believed is our only link to the Word that became flesh in the person of Jesus of Nazareth.

So despite all the cultural obstacles, we still rededicate ourselves to the mission of the living Word in our history, in our existence, in our society. So, what is the special burden of this mission of the Word in our time?

First of all, the mission of the Word is to liberate people from themselves and their own hang-ups . . . to get them to look beyond themselves. The office of the preacher is there to bring you a message not of your own making or liking. It is a Word that has been shaped in the events of history. It is a Word that does not come bubbling up out of your own experiences, not a Word that rises to the surface through consciousness-raising. It is a Word that comes from outside of us. As Luther said, Christianity is a Word that someone has to stick into your ear. Not the eye, not an inner light, and not by touching or tasting, but through the ear, through hearing we receive the Word of faith that means life and salvation . . . and then all these other senses make sense.

And secondly, the mission of the Word is to be our adversary. Strange thought, that we should need an adversary. Don't we have enemies enough? Aren't we all on somebody's enemy list? Aren't there enough harping voices, to accuse, to cut, and to beat us down? True indeed, but we need the righteous criticism of the Word that cuts away our pride; we need to be jostled into dialogue with transcendent justice. No person can be good, no team can rise to excellence, no assembly of sinners can become a fellowship of saints without stirring sharp criticism. The Word of Christ that we are called to proclaim is not always sweet and soft; certainly it is poles apart from Norman Vincent Peale's "power of positive thinking."

Several seasons ago when the Chicago Bears were losing one ball game after another, the coach invited W. Clement Stone to give the Bears a few lessons in his PMA technique—Positive Mental Attitude. After it all was over, the Bears said they felt better, they had a better attitude, but they went on losing. What they needed was something more radical than a more cheerful attitude in the course of losing. So it is with preaching the Word of God. The goal of preaching is not merely to make people feel better, not merely to soothe their feelings, not anything like transactional analysis or transcendental meditation, which only drives you more deeply into yourself, under the tyranny of your own inner nature and some personal scheme of self-salvation.

And finally, the mission of the Word, in addition to being our own undoing, bringing needed judgment and criticism, the mission of the Word is to bring forgiveness, life, and salvation, to bring the power of new being, to perform the miracle of being and becoming a believer in Jesus Christ and a member of his communion. This is the positive, freeing, healing, life-bestowing function of the Word of God. This is the loving, caring, and consoling word, the good news, overcoming all the bad news that the headlines throw at us. This is the word of resurrection beyond our having to die; this is life in the Spirit that brings hope to a suffering creation. This is what the people need to hear, and it is something they can't pull out of themselves. This is the Word that we dare to speak for Christ's sake, when we face problems of every sort, and the sheer monstrous verdict of imminent death robs us of speech. The encounter with death is the final test of the Word we hear, for it is death that makes us speechless. Death is the axe of annihilation poised above each one of us, and that makes the wisest philosophers stare into the abyss of nothingness or makes them mutter something vague about the immortality of the soul.

Whoever hears you, hears the voice of the Lord who lives, the Lord who rules over death, whose power is greater than the last enemy of mankind, and by whose resurrection the sting of death has been pulled for all those who believe. So in the last analysis, as ministers of the Word, we are advocates of the people who have been crushed by life, and like a lawyer, a defense attorney, we plead the cause of the people before the highest court, or better, as a priest, we intercede for the people, not in our own name, but in the name of the great High Priest, who became the mediator of eternal salvation to all who believe and obey.

It may be a difficult time to witness. We may have to swim against the streams. We may be tempted to give up and resort to gimmicks that promise to give the appearance of instant success and quick results. We may redefine and redesign the minister's role. But any congregation which silences the living Word in its midst is playing Russian roulette. I am sure that you realize that our role as a congregation of believers is to keep open the channels of proclamation in preaching and teaching, and to prepare the way of the Lord and to make his paths straight, through the Word and through faith.

As minister and people meet with intensity and fidelity around the Word, the biblical Word, the incarnate Word, the living Word of the Gospel, we will have found the common denominator of our unity and the driving force of our mission to the world. This loyalty to the Word that appeared in Christ can cleanse our polluted words so that as we proclaim, we may be etching this apostolic epitaph on our lives like so many in the succession before us, that great cloud of witnesses. Whoever hears you, hears Christ; whoever hears what you preach, the core message, is brought into contact with the living and liberating Word of the Gospel. There can be no greater aspiration, no greater achievement, than to be a link between the here and now of our lives and the original identity of God's Word that appeared in Jesus the Christ.

Treasure in Earthen Vessels

This is how one should regard us, as servants of Christ and stewards of the mysteries of God.
— 1 CORINTHIANS 4:1

But we have this treasure in earthen vessels, to show that the transcendent power belongs to God and not to us.
— 2 CORINTHIANS 4:7

Twenty five years ago the celebrated study of the Protestant ministry in our century, conducted by H. Richard Niebuhr, Daniel Day Williams and James M. Gustafson, dealt with the confusion among ministers about the purpose of the church and the role of their ministry. Niebuhr declared: "The contemporary church is confused about the nature of the ministry. Neither ministers nor the schools that nurture them are guided today by a clear-cut, generally accepted concept of the ministry." But, Niebuhr added, "such an idea may be emerging." That was when he launched his famous idea of the minister as "pastoral director."

Now twenty five years later we have just received a new mas-

114

sive social scientific study of *Ministry in America,* conducted by the Association of Theological Schools, and edited by David Schuller, Merton Strommen, and Milo Brekke. The conclusive result is that no clear-cut idea of the role of the minister in the American church has yet emerged. All the surveys indicated that the only constant in the ever-changing forms of ministry is the rate of change itself, leading to an acceleration of confusion. And this time around, we cannot say with the confidence of Niebuhr that a clear-cut generally accepted idea of the ministry is emerging.

In the 1950s you had to be stupid or lazy to be a failure in ministry, that period of Christian triumphalism, when our churches joined the gold rush to the suburbs, saw their memberships expand and budgets soar. Then we began to hear some bad news about the suburban captivity of the church, and to have second thoughts about using the message to massage the spiritual backs of those who pay their dues and come to our church parlors. If you consider the changes, from the church neurotic of the 1950s to the church electric of the '80s, you wonder what it is that has kept the veterans of ministry still going steadily in the right direction. For a lot of ministers, from their own confession, are like that pitiful dog in a crate left on the platform of a train station. A passenger noticing the dog with its forlorn appearance, exclaimed to a nearby railway attendant. "My, what an unhappy looking dog." The attendant agreed: "He is unhappy—very unhappy. The poor hound doesn't know where he's come from, or where he's at. And that's not the worst of it. He's chewed up his destination tag, so he doesn't know where he's bound for either."

In the 1950s we came out of the seminary armed with biblical theology and church dogmatics, and thought we knew what the ministry was all about. We believed what we preached and taught what we knew. That was the view from above—the pulpit view, which always stood about six feet above contradiction from the pew level below. We didn't solicit feed-back from the pew-sitters. But then a trickle of suspicion invaded our confidence with the proposition that our beautiful message, biblically and doctrinally sound, was not getting through. It may be ever so true, but if it's not getting through, then what's the good of it? This explains how we got on the merry-go-round in search of a ministry that works, a ministry that succeeds, a ministry that is relevant to the *real* needs of people and the *serious* problems of society.

It is common for old friends to inquire of each other, when they get together: "What are you into now?" I have known ministers who in one career of ministry have been into every new fangled phase of ministry that comes along. They have tried every latest formula for successful ministry as soon as it hits the market. There was the psychological phase—getting lots of counseling skills to help individuals cope with their feelings of guilt, anxiety, frustration, and inferiority. When it became clear that this individualistic psychological approach does not change the world, then there came the prophetic phase, when the problems of society—overpopulation, pollution, and poverty—were announced and denounced from the pulpit. And when it became clear that prophetic rhetoric doesn't change the structures of society, and ministers are not effective change agents, then there came a parting of ways. Some ministers simply quit, and began to sell life insurance to the ministers who didn't. Others went into radical politics, finding some para-parochial base from which to operate, either in a community organization or in a national church office, out of line of direct fire from the paying parishioners. And others took the trip eastward and inward—getting back into religious things, and into deep "spirituality." That's where lots of people are at who are still hanging on in ministry these days.

Even my good friend, Jürgen Moltmann, has lately been making noises to this effect. At a conference for ministers last year,

Moltmann declared: "What we need now are more ministers who are willing to take the inner journey, a trip into the inner spiritual life." To which one of the critic-respondents, a man who had been a missionary to India, queried: "Professor Moltmann, how many do you think we need?" And I would add, "What do we need them for?"

There are echoes of truth in all the experiences and experiments our generation of ministers tried in the fifties and sixties and seventies. We have this treasure in *earthen* vessels, and so like everything earthly the vessels of ministry are subject to time and history, change and decay, death and renewal. Where there is life, there is change; when things become static, they are dead.

And so we celebrate this treasure in earthen vessels. We have no heavenly vessels. God has always done it this way. He has always chosen things of his own earthly creation by means of which to meet us. His revelation comes in the events and stories of real history. His eternal Word became a little boy from Nazareth. His living Spirit dwells in a body all of whose members are sick unto death. The knowledge of salvation in Jesus Christ— that's a gift wrapped in the ancient languages of Hebrew and Greek. And folly of follies, God has chosen to speak to us in sermons so boring, that only the Holy Spirit working overtime can keep people inspired and enthusiastic about their Christian calling. And he comes to us in the earthly elements of bread and wine, most often unhealthy bread and bad tasting wine we'd prefer not to consume if we had any choice.

Treasure in earthen vessels! That's always been God's way. There are many times when we wonder: "O God, why did you choose a clod like me?" Earthen vessels, all of us! Cracked pots, most of us! What's God trying to prove? That the transcendent power belongs to him and not to us! We have this ministry of treasure in earthen vessels, by the power and grace of God.

People don't always necessarily want their vessels of ministry to be entirely earthen. We are all tempted to try to supernaturalize and to spiritualize our ministries a bit. When the Pharisees tried that, Jesus called them "white-washed sepulchres," glittering with a hallowed glow on the outside, rotten with vermin on the inside. According to the *Ministry in America* study, lay people want a super-pastor. The truly successful pastor in our culture is a celebrity. If you put your heart on those desires and expectations, you will have to reach the top five percent to find satisfaction in the ordained ministry. But if we want to be servants of the Christ whose pulpit is the cross, we may not necessarily reap much success in ministry. The ministry is not a stepping stone to personal glory and self-fulfillment.

The earthen vessels come in all sizes and shapes and colors and sounds, in every class and race and gender and dialect. But what's the treasure inside? It is the "gospel of the glory of Christ, who is the likeness of God" (2 Cor. 4:4). It is "the light of the knowledge of the glory of God in the face of Christ" (2 Cor. 4:6). Is that all? Nothing but Christ? Isn't there something else as well, something more glorious that sells better than the gospel of salvation in Christ's name alone? Aren't there some secular substitutes and religious supplements that might satisfy the people more, and help to bring them in? It seems so psychologically narrow, it seems so intellectually inexplicable, and so culturally gauche, to take all this education, and throw it away in the cause of a purely gratuitous affair, which the world never asked for, doesn't believe it needs, and is not willing to pay for.

As an ordinand, you are being inducted into an international union of stewards of the mysteries of God. That's it. Martin Luther's dad wanted him to be a lawyer. I've talked to seminarians who have told me a similar story, how they've been made to feel shame for disappointing their dad for seeking the vocation of ministry when they could have been a lawyer, they could have been a doctor, or a success in business.

In one of his ninety five theses, Luther declared: "The true treasure of the church is the Holy Gospel of the glory and grace of God. This treasure, however, is deservedly most hateful, because it makes the last to be first." It is because Luther had his heart and mind on this treasure, that he could say in words that we now pass on: "Whoever has the office of preaching imposed on him has the highest office in Christendom imposed on him." As one of the stewards in a great succession of stewards in the economy of God's plan of salvation, you will be given the key to the house, a key to open up the treasure chest filled with the mysteries of God.

And after today, what shall we call you? What shall we call a person who takes up the ministry of Christ to his people and the world? People are title-conscious, you know, and ministers are people. Or why do ministers want to be called "doctor" and what's all the fuss about in changing from president to bishop? I have just read a proposal that a Lutheran minister is essentially a priest. Maybe that sounds better, religiously more high-falutin than just plain pastor. One of the high churchmen of our Lutheran tradition has stated, however, in his essay "Concerning the Ministry:" "We neither can nor ought to give the name priest to those who are in charge of Word and Sacrament among the people. The reason they have been called priests is either because of the custom of heathen people or as a vestige of the Jewish nation. The result is greatly injurious to the church. According to the New Testament Scriptures better names would be ministers, deacons, bishops, stewards, presbyters. For thus St. Paul wrote, 'This is how one should regard us, as servants of Christ and stewards of the mysteries of God.'" The name of that high churchman is Martin Luther.

You are to be a fully accredited and authorized steward in the household of the family that God has assembled in the name of Christ, who himself is the chief steward. You will now be put in charge of the treasures of the gospel, in charge of all that God has given to us for Christ's sake. That's the only authority you will have, unless you grab some that doesn't belong to the stewards of the house. This authority is entrusted to you as one of the stewards, free to deal in behalf of the master of the house. Doctors and lawyers don't have this authority. Presidents and generals don't have this authority. People of business and finance don't have this kind of authority. We have this ministry, this authority, strictly by the mercy of God. And for this reason we can shout with Paul, "We do not lose heart."

Marriage: What a Mystery!

*For this reason a man shall leave his father and mother
and be joined to his wife, and the two shall become one.
This is a great mystery, and I take it to mean Christ and
the church.* —EPHESIANS 5:31-32

Paul says that marriage is a mystery. To call something a mystery suggests that its meaning lies deeper than we are ordinarily prone to think. Perhaps everybody thinks they know about the meaning of marriage. It's no secret. It has the obvious meaning of tying a man and a woman together in a social contract. It has the natural meaning of fulfilling a deep desire and longing of a man and a woman to become intimately united in love permanently and profoundly. At this obvious natural level we all know pretty much the same things about marriage. You can read about it in any marriage manual. You don't need a priest or a pastor, you don't need the Bible or the church, to tell you about this obvious natural social and human meaning of marriage. Nowadays they teach all this in the schools. But Paul says marriage is a mystery. To say it is a mystery is to say that its meaning, its deeper meaning, has to be revealed. A mystery is a purely natural event that points to a supernatural meaning.

What makes it a mystery? It is a mystery because it points to the union of Christ with his church. That is the essence of the Christian marriage. Your very natural desire to leave your separate states and to become one, is a sign pointing to the deeper unity of Christ and his church.

This means that your unity is not an isolated unity. It is linked to the mystery of Christ and his church. This is so important, because many forces in the life you face together will try to tear you apart. Especially in the modern marriage, we see so much brokenness, fragmentation, dividedness, divorce. So you will need the reinforcement of unity which the grace of God in Christ and his church can bring you. We are saying that you don't have to begin your life together merely on your own strength and resources. We can promise you the grace and power of unity we have in Christ and his church.

This unity is not something that just happens automatically and lasts forever. The unity of marriage needs to be nourished and sustained by love and forgiveness. Your marriage can run for awhile on feelings and emotions, but sooner or later it must be anchored in something more solid. And nothing is more solid than the rock of unity we have in Christ and the fellowship of believers in him.

In America today, many people are trying to go it alone, and before long they go separately to the divorce courts, cursing and accusing each other. But we have this mystery of a deep bond of unity with Christ and his church, and we can build our marriages not on the sinking sand of our own feelings and emotions, but on the granite-foundation of Christ who promises to be with us always even until the end.

Marriage is a mystery. That means it is so profound, you will never exhaust its meaning. You will discover that marriage is something more than adding two persons together and more than living together. People may become stale to each other and routine in their actions, but if there is a real marriage, we can never get to the bottom of this mystery. Every year, every day is a new exploration into the meaning of the mystery of marriage. That is because we are not merely exploring ourselves. There is more to life than that. We are exploring and probing the depth of the meaning of life lived before the face of God. In marriage we receive a partner, a close companion, to share the wonderful mystery of life lived not for ourselves, but for God and in the service of our fellow humans.

Responsible Love

For this reason a man shall leave his father and mother and be joined to his wife, and the two shall become one. This is a great mystery, and I take it to mean Christ and the church.

—EPHESIANS 5:31-32

Paul himself finds the heart of this mystery in that love concerning which he wrote in 1 Corinthians: "Love is patient and kind; love is not jealous or boastful; it is not arrogant or rude. Love does not insist on its own way; it is not irritable or resentful; it does not rejoice at wrong, but rejoices in the right. Love bears all things, believes all things, hopes all things, endures all things. Love never ends."

Love is the heart of the mystery of all life. There is a mystery; people cannot decide to fall in love. It happens or it doesn't happen. It's like a miracle. But they do *decide* whether or not to place that love into an exclusive, life-long partnership of marriage. That is a vocation. So a person falls in love, but intentionally steps forward into marriage. It is a decision; it is a

125

promise; it is an act of commitment, responsibility and fulfillment through mutual sacrifice.

But marriage is not only, and certainly not always, a warm nest where two little love-birds can escape into a delirium of peace and joy. We do not only bring our love and idealism into marriage. We bring ourselves, our selfish, jealous, arrogant, rude, insensitive, and irresponsible selves into the partnership. The Bible tells us that marriage, as everything else, is overcast by sin. Because of sin marriage so easily becomes a battlefield of wills, both partners out to get their share, each one shifting the blame on the other, each one using the other to reach their own private goals. It is so easy for love to break down, and for marriage to degenerate into envy, suspicion, boredom, even violence and murder.

Those are two factors: First, God has created men and women for love and marriage, and that's good. He has created us for sharing and partnership; that's very good. But second, all of this good has been overcast by sin, and that's the way it is. Those are givens! We all start from there. But that's not the whole story. Thank God! The rest of the story must be filled in by each one of us, completed by the new possibilities of life which our Christian faith makes available to the two of us. We do not have to be destroyed and defeated by sin. There is power in the great mystery; there is magic in that love which makes it possible for one plus one to equal one; so that the two persons become one flesh and a harmony of two wills.

Loving enough to get married is just the beginning. The next step is to grow in responsibility. Responsible love. That's what we all need in our marriage and family life, taking responsibility for the other person! This responsible love is not encouraged by the fashionable trends of our day and the spirit of the age. Christian marriage is going against the stream of our culture. The mystery in successful marriage is living for the other, living for the fulfillment of the other. The modern folly is to get married in a quest for self-fulfillment; to stay married only as long as it seems fulfilling, as long as the other person can be a useful means in my own personal quest for fulfillment. That view of marriage has divorce built into it as the escape hatch.

As Christians you are free to hold views contrary to the spirit of the age, taking your values from the Scriptures and from Christ and his church, and not from Hollywood and popular magazines and the trends of the times. This means that you will keep and nourish the great mystery at the center of your marriage; you will act toward each other as Christ has acted toward the church. Your marriage will be a supreme instance of the love that surrenders and sacrifices for the fulfillment and well-being of the other. You will be doing on a small scale what Christ has done on a large scale, pouring out his life that the world might live. You will pour out your lives for each other, not grasping what you can get for yourself. You will find joy in that old-fashioned virtue of self-sacrifice, not seeking the indulgence of your own desires. You will practice the secret which our Lord broke to us: The person who loses his life in living for the other, doing what Christ has done for us, will find the meaning of life, the meaning also of that great mystery which lies at the heart of marriage.